HUMAN RIGHT ISSUES AND WOMEN IN INFORMAL SECTOR

HUMAN RIGHT ISSUES AND WOMEN IN INFORMAL SECTOR

By

Dr. Shashi A. Mishra

Head

Department of Sociology

Ramniranjan Jhunjhunwala College

Mumbai (Maharashtra)

(India)

DISCOVERY PUBLISHING HOUSE PVT. LTD.

NEW DELHI-110 002

Published by:
Tilak Wasan

DISCOVERY PUBLISHING HOUSE PVT. LTD.
4383/4A, Ansari Road, Darya Ganj
New Delhi-110 002 (India)
Phone : +91-11-23279245, 43596064-65
Fax : +91-11-23253475
E-mail : parul.wasan@gmail.com
discoverypublishinghouse@gmail.com
web : www.discoverypublishinggroup.com

First Edition: **2012**
ISBN: 978-93-5056-100-3

Human Right Issues and Women in Informal Sector

Printed at:
Shree Balaji Art Press
Delhi

Acknowledgement

It is my privilege to express my deep sense of gratitude to my friends and well wishers of mine for extending their full support and co-operation. The strongest support has come from the Principal Dr. (Mrs.) Usha Mukundan and staff of R.J.College, Ghatkopar, where I work. Dr.(Mrs) Usha Mukundan has not only given me institutional support, but was a source of inspiration for completing this work. Many people stood by me during this period and all names cannot be mentioned.

I would like to thank the Almighty for his grace and blessings in all my activities.

I would like to thank my guide Dr. P.G. Jogdand, for his inspiration, constant encouragement and guidance which enabled me to complete the research successfully.

I gratefully acknowledge the assistance given to me by the library staff of Jawaharlal Nehru Library, SNDT University Library and Ramniranjan Jhunjhunwala college library.

I also wish to express my thanks to my family, for all the encouragement and support given to me.

At last accord my serious thanks to Mr. Tilak Wasan, Director, Discovery Publishing House Pvt. Ltd., for expediting the publication of this book.

Dr. Shashi A Mishra

Contents

Introduction

Definition of Human Rights

Human rights are rights inherent to all human beings, whatever their nationality, place of residence, sex, national or ethnic origin, colour, religion, language, or any other status. We are all equally entitled to our human rights without discrimination. These rights are all interrelated, interdependent and indivisible. Universal human rights are often expressed and guaranteed by law, in the forms of treaties, customary international law, general principles and other sources of international law. International human rights law lays down obligations of Governments to act in certain ways or to refrain from certain acts, in order to promote and protect human rights and fundamental freedoms of individuals or groups.

It has been observed that human beings everywhere around the world demand the realisation of diverse values or capabilities to ensure their individual and collective well-being. Also this demand is often painfully frustrated by social as well as natural forces, resulting in exploitation, oppression, persecution, and other forms of deprivation. Deeply rooted in these twin observations are the beginnings of what today is called 'human rights' and the national and international legal processes that are associated with them.

The term 'human rights' is relatively new, having come into everyday parlance only since World War II, the founding of the United Nations in 1945, and the adoption by the UN General Assembly of the Universal Declaration of Human Rights in 1948. It replaced the phrase 'natural rights,' which fell into disfavour in part because the concept of natural law (to which it was intimately linked) had become a matter of great controversy; and it replaced as well the later phrase 'the rights of Man,' which was not universally understood to include the rights of women.[1]

A large number of urban centers have emerged all round the world in the process of industrialization and urbanization, this in turn has lead to lot of infrastructure development. In the era of liberalization and globalization, due to higher rate of economic growth, the construction sector too has got a boost. Similar impact of infrastructure development and increase in construction work has taken place in different parts of India. Both the processes i.e. industrialization and urbanization, involve heavy construction work. Factory buildings, accessory and ancillary buildings, government offices, roads, railway tracks and Entire Township need to be erected and constructed. Irrespective of occasional slumps in the economy or in construction works, the sector is going through a faster growth. Apart from old / traditional urban/ industrial centre, new industrial/urban centre have appeared on the map where construction works are going on large scale. Expanding and fast growing construction sector and in general, lack of greater employment opportunity elsewhere has drawn large number of workers in this sector.

In developing country like India, rapid technological change, expanding globalization, profound cultural shifts and new economic trends have brought cultural shifts and new economic trends have brought about a whole range of fresh opportunities and challenges. With liberalization of economy, Private sector participation has also given a boost to development in various sectors.

Construction Industry is one such sector which has gained a lot of importance due to the emergence of a number of urban centers in our country as a result of industrialization and Urbanization. Major changes have occurred in these industries due to rapid mechanization and as an outcome, unemployment has increased and women workers have turned on to construction as an alternative source of income generation. The construction industry is one of the largest and oldest industry to be generating employment in India, next to the agriculture sector.

Emergence of International Bill of Human Rights

Human rights is a fairly new name for what were formerly called natural rights and the rights of man. While examining the historical evolution of human rights is beyond the scope of this thesis it could be noted that its origin can be traced back primarilty to the thinkers of the 17th and 18th centuries. Philosophers such as Hobbes, Descartes, Leibniz, Spinoza, Bacon and Locke encouraged a belief in natural law and universal order. During the 18th century, the so-called Age of Enlightenment, a growing confidence in human reason and in the perfectibility of human affairs led to the more comprehensive expression of this belief. Locke argued in detail, mainly in writings associated with the English Glorious Revolution (1688), that certain rights self-evidently pertain to individuals as human beings (because these rights existed in 'the state of nature' before humankind entered civil society); that chief among them are the rights to life, liberty (freedom from arbitrary rule), and property; that, upon entering civil society, humankind surrendered to the state—pursuant to a 'social contract'—only the right to enforce these natural rights and not the rights themselves; and that the state's failure to secure these rights gives rise to a right to responsible, popular revolution. Revolutionary people vigorously attacked religious and scientific dogmatism, intolerance, censorship, and social and economic restraints.[2]

The Glorious Revolution in England and the resulting Bill of Rights, provided the rationale for the wave of revolutionary agitation in North America and France. In 17th century the Declaration of Independence, proclaimed by the 13 American colonies on July 4, 1776: "We hold these truths to be self-evident, that all men are created equal, that they are endowed by their Creator with certain unalienable Rights, that among these are Life, Liberty and the Pursuit of Happiness." Similarly, the Marquis de Lafayette, who won the close friendship of George Washington and who shared the hardships of the American Revolution, imitated the pronouncements of the English Declaration of Independence and American revolutions in the Declaration of the Rights of Man and of the Citizen of August 26, 1789, proclaiming that "...men are born and remain free and equal in rights..." and that "the aim of every political association is the preservation of the natural and imprescriptibly rights of man."

The first generation of civil and political rights derives primarily from the 17th and 18th century reformist theories noted above. The first generation favours the abstention of the intervention of government in the quest for human dignity, includes freedom from gender, racial and equivalent forms of discrimination, the right to life, liberty and security of the person; freedom from slavery or involuntary servitude; freedom from torture and from cruel, inhuman, or degrading treatment or punishment; freedom from arbitrary arrest, detention, or exile; the right to a fair and public trial; freedom from interference in privacy and correspondence; freedom of movement and residence; the right to asylum from persecution; freedom of thought, conscience, and religion; freedom of opinion and expression; freedom of peaceful assembly and association; and the right to participate in government, directly or through free elections. Also included are the right to own property and the right not to be deprived of it arbitrarily – rights that were fundamental to the interests fought for in the American and French revolutions and to the rise of capitalism. The provisions of the classical Bill of Rights, as contained in the first ten amendments to the U.S. Constitution or in the first explicit declaration of rights, adopted by the revolutionary French National Assembly in 1789, can be considered as the origins of the first generation of civic and personal rights and liberties. Apart from rights concerning the protection of personal integrity, including freedom of belief and religion, these rights, now enshrined and elaborated in articles 1-21 of UDHR, also encompass the right to participate in public affairs.[3]

The second generation of economic, social, and cultural rights originated primarily from within the socialist tradition, in France in 19th century and promoted by revolutionary struggles and welfare movements. In large part, it is a response to the abuses of capitalist development and its underlying and essentially uncritical conception of individual liberty, which tolerated, and even legitimised, the exploitation of working classes and colonial peoples. Historically, it is a counterpoint to the first generation of civil and political rights, conceiving of human rights more in positive terms ('rights to') than in negative ones ('freedoms from') and requiring more the intervention than the abstention of the state for the purpose of assuring the equitable production and distribution of the values or capabilities involved. The 'second generation' of rights is concerned with guaranteeing and safeguarding precisely the pre-conditions for exercising this and related rights effectively. Articles 22-28 of Universal Declaration of Human Rights (UDHR) are concerned with social rights, including the individual's right to work, but they also contain provisions on the level both of the individual nation state and on that of the international order for state action to ensure a decent living for their citizens. Active citizenship would be a meaningless and empty shell without such provisions to ensure the individuals a minimum measure of material conditions, free from the immediate concern of bare survival.[4]

Article 28 of UDHR expands this principle, going beyond the confines of the national state and calling for an adequate social and international order. Along these lines, international human rights' instruments have been developed after the adoption of UDHR by the UN General Assembly in 1948. These include, besides the international pacts on civic and social rights, the declarations on the Right to Peace and the Right to Development, referred to as 'third generation Human Rights'. The defining feature of these rights are that they are group rights as against the predominantly individual based rights included in the first and second generation rights.[5]

Thus, at various stages of modern history, the content of human rights has been broadly defined not with any expectation that the rights associated with one generation would or should become outdated upon the ascendancy of another, but expansively or supplementally. The history of the content of human rights reflects evolving perceptions of which values or capabilities stand, at different times, most in need of responsible attention and, simultaneously, humankind's recurring demands for continuity and stability. In this thesis we will focus primarily on one of the rights that is often considered to be a second generation rights, namely right to livelihood. It is to this aspect that we will focus in the next section.

Right to Livelihood as a Right

Livelihoods for people are a means to live a life with dignity. Right to Livelihood is a terminology which is gaining momentum .It can be defined as 'Right the right to earn with dignity and respect'. As per Lord Buddha's writing Right to livelihood is connected with first defining what right livelihood is i.e. Livelihood without killing living beings, livelihood earned through honesty, Livelihood through dignity.[6]

Right to livelihood has been promoted by international organisations such as the United Nations (UN), International Labour Organisation (ILO), and United Nations International Children's Education Fund (UNICEF). The Human Right to Livelihood includes the following universal, indivisible, interconnected and interdependent human rights:

- The human right to livelihood and work that is freely chosen and that contributes to an adequate standard of living.
- The human right to basic labour protections; freedom of association; freedom from forced labour; adequate, safe working conditions; equal pay for equal work.
- The human right to freedom from discrimination based on gender, race, ethnic identity, or any other status.
- The human right to full equality before the law.
- The human right to equal access to productive resources, including land, credit, and technology.
- The human right to equal access to education and training.

The main purpose of these efforts is to protect the rights of the workers in general and those of women in particular as they are among the most vulnerable sections of the society. These guidelines are to apply to all workers including those working in the informal sector.

Since then early 1970's the notion of labour in the developing countries is dominated by a dichotomy in terms of formal and informal sector workers. A sizeable section of labourers find themselves at the bottom of society without any kind of job security and regularity of the employment. They work for long hours without much productivity enhancing skills or technology; they remain by and large extremely poor with regard to basic subsistence as well as a dignified human existence. Their position at the bottom is reinforced by strong social segmentation such as caste or community identity in this societies.[7]

In today's socio-economic and political environment, people's livelihoods are threatened in various ways. Development projects, focuses more on infrastructure development resulting in mass displacements, environmental degradation and destruction of natural resources. In addition sustainable forms of agriculture are disappearing. Disasters, man-made or natural are worsening the situation. Women perennially suffer the most. Such events lead to mass migration, hardship and exploitation. The global phenomena of using women labour as cheap option to substitute development investment and targeting women resource for development and profit is rapidly increasing. As a result people, especially women from backward class are pushed away from self reliant sources of livelihood to dependency on others business which lead to poverty exploitation and basic human rights violation.

It is in view of this increased violation of right to livelihood that an organisation Programme on Women's Economic, Social and Cultural Rights (PWESCR) in partnership with several organizations globally has initiated a international Network on Women's Right to livelihood. The goal of this group is to emphasise that it is the right of everyone to earn an adequate standard of living for himself and his family, including adequate food, clothing and housing, and to the continuous improvement of living conditions." While this provision is sometimes interpreted as 'the right to work', the group has expanded its analysis to include the right to livelihood, which focuses on the conditions that are necessary to support, sustain, and advance the lives of women and their families in dignity.[8]

In India, the Constitution has described Right to Livelihood as integral facet to life. For millions of Indians who live below the poverty line, the right to life will be of no significance if they do not have right to livelihood. The state is under the obligation under article 39(a) of the constitution, to provide, promote and protect the life or the right to livelihood or the right to exist. It is an age old principle that "a life cannot be extinguished or taken away except according to the procedure established by law". The other fact of the principle is "no person can live without the means of livelihood". The Supreme Court expanded the reach and ambit of Article 21 and ruled that the word 'life' in Article 21 includes the 'right to livelihood' also. It does not mean merely that life cannot be extinguished or taken away as, for example, by the imposition and execution of death sentence, except according to procedure established by law. This is but one aspect of the right to life. An equally important facet of that right is the right to livelihood because no person can live in a dignified manner without a source of income. If the right to livelihood is not treated as part of constitutional right to life, the easiest ways of depriving a person of his right to life would be to deprive him of his means of livelihood".[9]

Over five decades after the independence, numerous efforts have been made by the government of India and civil society organizations to ameliorate the condition of women in various spheres of life. The main purpose was to raise their status in society, economy, polity and education, thereby according them equality, vis-à-vis their male counterparts.

Despite many efforts, large segments of the women population continue to be deprived of their basic human rights, i.e., the right to own property and wealth as compared to men (e.g. in patriarchal society after death of father/husband the right over the property goes to son and not to daughter or wife). Deprivation from this singular important reality of existence has kept women powerless for centuries and millennia. As a result, today their condition and status still remain much below the desired level in the context of democratic participation in all spheres of human activities which have been postulated in the constitutional framework of the country and pronouncements in the different international fora. Therefore, the major issues which concern women are their unequal status at large and in the areas of education, employment, political participation, health, etc. Discrimination against women is deep-rooted and rampant. It begins much before her birth. The shameful phenomenon of foeticide is a most heinous form of discriminatory violence perpetuated against her. In day to day life, she undergoes many forms of violence within and outside her home.

The main idea is to highlight the fact that even though all conventions and recommendations adopted by ILO are applicable to both men and women workers. But there are some standards of particular relevance to women workers such as: concern for equal remuneration, discrimination in employment, maternity protection, night work of women, underground work, occupational health and safety measures etc. which are practically not followed or practiced by informal sector. In construction business the researcher has attempted to highlight this point that women workers are not treated properly and rights of women workers has been violated. Despite of efforts through various organisation women workers in construction industry are deprived of their basic human rights.

Hypotheses

The major hypotheses that are sought to be verified in the study are :

- Some of the basic human rights mentioned in CEDAW and the Indian constitution such as right to equality, equal pay for equal work, right to health care, maternity benefits are denied to women working in the construction industry. Wage discrimination between man and woman continue to exist in construction industry.
- There is an unfair division of labour based on gender.
- There is a direct relation of poverty and migration of the workers in the construction sector.

- Women still suffer from sexual exploitation and are not aware of the various protective labour legislations enacted for their benefit.

Objectives

The present study seeks to understand working conditions and conditions of work of women in construction sites from a human rights perspective. The important objectives of the present study are:

1. To study the socio-economic profile of the women workers engaged in construction industry.
2. To examine the factors compelling women to undertake construction work.
3. To study the problems faced working women in the construction industry while managing the dual responsibility of housewife and construction worker.
4. To study the working relationship between the contractors, builders and the female employees.
5. To explore the conditions of work such as wages, hours of work, leaves, holidays, bonus, overtime, incentives, etc in the construction industry of Bhandup area.
6. To investigate and observe the working conditions such as health, sanitation, safety and welfare etc of the female workers in this industry. To know the level of awareness of the women workers on the trade unions operating in the area.
7. To examine whether these women know their rights and are able to assert them.

Methodology

The study depended upon primary and secondary sources. In the present study, the data has been collected from the selected respondents with the help of structured interview scheduled specially designed for the purpose. Besides employers some significant persons like mukadams and contractors were also consulted to gather further information concerning the problem. Spot observations and discussions were also used for verifying the information collected from the women respondents in the field.

Interview scheduled for women workers was designed and utilised for collecting the data from the field. The schedule was designed according to the objectives of the study. The questions were drafted in English language but in the course of field visits, these questions were translated into Hindi. The framing of such questions was done in such a way that the respondents could easily understand and respond. At times while administering the interview schedule to the respondents, informal discussions on various aspects also took place and these anecdotal information provided some useful inputs.

The interview gave an opportunity to the researcher to have a face to face interaction with the respondents. The permission of those being interviewed was sought and the confidentiality of the respondent was maintained. A few of the respondents were interviewed in presence of their husbands because they were reluctant to be talked alone.

After the interview was over, all the information was checked and some were rewritten against the appropriate choices of a particular question so as to facilitate subsequent analysis of the data. Simple statistical methods like average ratios and percentage were used at appropriate places for analysing the data.

The researcher has made use of secondary resources such as books, journals, reports, newspaper articles in libraries of University of Mumbai, the Departmental library of Department of Civics and Politics, University of Mumbai, Shreemati Nathibai Damodar Thackersey Women's University (Juhu), Tata institute of Social Science and Akshara,.

Review of Literature

Status of women varies enormously from one part of the world to another. A review of the studies of women at large and women workers in particular brings forth the point that studies on the women in unorganised sector are limited and these studies do not cover many aspects of the problems faced by women employed in this sector. Hence to have better understanding of women role in urban informal sector, review of literature has been useful to an extent to buildup the current study.

K.D. Gangrade and J.A. Gathia in their book *Women And Child Workers in Unorganised Sector* have examined the problems faced by social workers, policy-makers and administration in promoting women and child development programmes. As we all know working children and women in the unorganised sector consist of sizeable numbers, their problems and difficulties does not receive proper/adequate attention of policy makers, planners, administration and legal luminaries. There are some devoted and voluntary organizations, which help them to solve their problem in whatever small way possible. The book raised questions instead of solutions. There are lot of inputs, which can help in designing more effective welfare policies and programmes for working women and children. This book also is very helpful in providing the relevant necessary data, in-depth discussion of the issues women and child workers in India.

Nandita Gandhi and Nandita Shah in their book *Shadow Workers – Women in Home-based Production* analyses the recent trend in work retrenchment, which leads to poverty, homelessness, and various problems. So to fulfill family needs more and more family members including small children are going out to work. The book highlights upon the zero involvement of trade Unions in the Informal Sector. One of the main reason was that historically trade unions have emerged wherever there is factory system where bad conditions of work and systematic increase in production of product has been taken place. The collective force of workmen was so big that bargaining power gave additional edge over the Owners. Unions also have ignored the informal sector workers as they are often used as strike breakers. The government only responds to group or political pressure. In absence of both in informal sector Trade union and government involvement is negligible. The researcher has tried to stress upon the need of government intervention in improving the conditions of women construction worker by at least ensuring that the basic human rights issues like medical facility, safety factors, basic hygiene factor etc are provided by builders.

The book *Women Workers in the Unorganised Sector* by Nirmala Banerjee highlights the working conditions of women in the unorganised sector in Kolkata and also tries to throw light on the suffering and exploitation by a large extent against those who are working in the unorganized sector. She further highlights that majority of them are domestic servants and the rest were doing unskilled and semiskilled jobs. About 25 per cent of them were working as piece rate workers and many of them were ready to work even in social tabooed areas.

Building Your Dreams; Women in the Construction Industry; Lahore, Pakistan by Yameena Mitha, is based on the study carried out on the conditions of women in the construction industry in Lahore, Pakistan. The book gives us a clear picture of the conditions prevalent in the working environment of the female workers in the mining and construction industry. It focuses on the problems specially related to work-long hours, unhealthy nature of work, physical hazards, neglect of housework and maternal duties.

This book has also tried to examine the nature of facilities required—medical, maternity leave and child care facilities, transportation and accommodation but has not tried to highlight the human labour laws and has failed in developing a suitable framework for labour standards in feminist perspectives.

The present review of the studies about woman workers in unorganised sector are very few, and do not cover every aspect of problems and conditions to these workers. The study on women worker in construction site are almost non-existence and those that exists are very sketchy and has not been done from the human rights perspective. The present study intends to explore a wide range of issues ranging from socio economic conditions, family life, trade unionism, living conditions of women workers of unorganized sector specially rights of women in construction industry.

REFERENCES

1. Claude, R. P., and Burns, H.W. (Eds.), *Human Rights in the World Community: Issues and Action,* University of Pennsylvania Press, Philadelphia, 1989.
2. Levin, Leah, *Human Rights: Questions and Answers*, National Book Trust, India , Mumbai, 1998.
3. Brysk Alison (Ed.), *Globalisation and Human Rights,* University of California Press, Berkely, 2002.
4. *Ibid.*
5. Coicaud, Jean Marc, and *et.al.*, *Globalisation of Human Rights*, Rawat Publications, Jaipur, 2004.
6. Yin-shun, *The Way to Buddhahood,* Wisdom Publications, Somerville, 2006.
7. ILO-WEP: *Informal Sector and Urban Employment: A Review of activities in the Urban Informal Sector,* International Labour Office, Geneva, 1990.
8. Progamme of Women and Economical, Social and Cultural Rights (PWESCR), *Partnering Organisation*, PWESCR, New Delhi, 2008
9. Chauhan O. P., and Dadwal, Lalit, *Human Rights Promotion and Protection* , Anmol Publishers, New Delhi, 2004.

Women's Right and the Informal Sector

Emergence of Women's Rights

Women constitute half of the human race in the world. In India, almost half of the population consisits of women. One hundred years ago, i.e., in 1901 the total female population of the country was 117.4 million. The figure rose to 494.82 million in 2001, thus accounting for 48.27 per cent of the total population. For millennia women of our society, like any other society, have suffered considerable deprivation and injustice in various spheres of life.[1]

The campaign for giving greater priority to women's rights gathered momentum in the 1970s with the proclaiming of 1975 as the International Women's Year, followed by a Women's Decade and the holding of world conferences on women. The most important thing that came out of the decade was the Convention on the Elimination of Discrimination Against Women (CEDAW).

Convention on the Elimination of Discrimination Against Women

In 1974 the Economic and Social Council appointed a 15 member Working Group to consider drafting a women's convention. In 1976, the Commission on Status of Women (CSW) took up the draft convention prepared by the working group with the objective of having a convention ready for the 1980 World Conference on Women in Copenhagen. Although suggestions were made to delay completion of the text for another year, the Convention on the Elimination of All Forms of Discrimination against Women was adopted by the General Assembly in 1979 by votes of 130 to none, with 10 abstentions. In resolution 34/180, in which the General Assembly adopted the Convention, the Assembly expressed the hope that the Convention would come into force at an early date and requested the Secretary-General to present the text of the Convention to the mid-decade World Conference of the United Nations Decade for Women.

At the special ceremony that took place at the Copenhagen Conference on 17 July 1980, 64 States signed the Convention and two States submitted their instruments of ratification. On 3 September 1981, 30 days after the twentieth member State had ratified it, the Convention entered into force—faster than any previous human rights convention had done. In 1979, the General Assembly adopted the Convention and opened it for signature and ratification. The Convention came into force on 3rd September having received 20 ratifications. Often described as the international bill rights for women, 185 states are as of 2009 (i.e. 90 per cent of the members of the UN) party to CEDAW. Consisting of a preamble and 30 articles, CEDAW defines what constitutes discrimination against women and sets up agenda for national action to end such discrimination.

The preamble to the Convention states that despite the affirmation of equal rights of men and women in the UN Charter, the UDHR and the International Covenants, extensive discrimination against women continues to exist. Critics have highlighted that it is ironical that the international community decided that the solution to the problem of violation of women's rights protected by human rights instruments lay in creating another international instrument. However, despite these criticisms, CEDAW has definitely been a step forward in protection of women's rights.

The Convention is divided into six parts. The first part (Articles 1-6) defines discrimination and broadly outlines the nature of state obligations, in terms of law, policy and programmes that the state needs to undertake in order to eliminate discrimination. Article defines discrimination as "... any distinction, exclusion or restriction made on the basis of sex which has the effect or purpose of impairing or nullifying the recognition, enjoyment or exercise by women, irrespective of their marital status, on a basis of equality of men and women, of human rights and fundamental freedoms in the political, economic, social cultural, civil or any other field." By formulating such a comprehensive definition of 'discrimination,' the convention provides a fundamental basis for eliminating discrimination. Gender inequalities exist, because of discrimination in the family and societal institutions, and social, cultural, and religious norms that perpetuate stereotypes, practices and beliefs that are detrimental to women. Human rights conventions provide redress for discrimination.

Part II of the Convention deals with rights of women in the political and public arena. It also grants to women equal rights to their nationality and the nationality of their children (Article 9 (1) (2)).

Part III of the Convention contains the rights to education (Article 10), employment (Article 11), health care and family planning (Article 12), economic and social benefit (Article 13). It also focuses on the problems faced by rural women and calls on state parties to eliminate discrimination against women in rural areas. (Article 14).

Part IV of the Convention deals with legal and civil rights. Article 15 grants women equality before law. Article 16 (1) calls upon state parties to eliminate discrimination against women in all matters relating to marriage and family relations. Article 16(2) prohibits child marriage.

Part V of the Convention establishes a Committee on the Elimination of Discrimination Against Women (CEDAW Committee) to monitor the progress made in the implementation of the Convention. Articles 17-22 detail the establishment and functions of the CEDAW Committee.

Part VI (Articles 23-30) deals largely with administrative and other procedural aspects of the Convention.

By accepting the Convention, States commit themselves to undertake a series of measures to end discrimination against women in all forms, including:

- to incorporate the principle of equality of men and women in their legal system, abolish all discriminatory laws and adopt appropriate ones prohibiting discrimination against women;
- to establish tribunals and other public institutions to ensure the effective protection of women against discrimination; and
- to ensure elimination of all acts of discrimination against women by persons, organizations or enterprises.

Feminist have often argued that though CEDAW is a well-meaning effort to recognise and protect women's rights, it has perpetuated the tendency to treat women's concerns as separate from general human rights concerns. The charge that women's issues are ghettoized' within the United Nations system needs to be viewed in the context that the classic human rights instruments were developed before feminists bought women's concerns to the attention of the international community. There is a growing recognition that women's issues are not separate from the mainstream human rights movement but are a specialised area of the movement. However, the greatest challenge before CEDAW Committee lies in not creating a parallel universe' for women but in bringing gender issues in the mainstream of the human rights agenda.[2]

CEDAW and India

India ratified CEDAW in 1993 but made reservations on the articles relating to cultural and customary practices (5 (a)) and to equality in marriage and family relations (16(1)).

In response to questions on India's First Report on CEDAW, the Secretary, Department of Women and Child Development, stated that international conventions and treaties ratified by India do not automatically form part of Indian law and need to be incorporated into Indian law through enabling legislation before implementation and enforcement of their provisions. The principal of gender equality is firmly established in the Indian Constitution.

Despite the constitutional safeguards and legislative provisions, discrimination against women is endemic. In order to ensure that legal and constitutional safeguards actually reach women, the government set up a statutory National Commission for Women in 1992, charged with the responsibility of overseeing the working of such safeguards and reviewing laws and regulations which are discriminatory to women. In response to question by CEDAW Committee on the measures taken by the Indian government to popularise CEDAW, the Secretary, Department of Women and Child Development, informed that the CEDAW text has been circulated widely to various ministries and departments. Sensitisation workshops have been held by national level institutions such as National Institute for Public Cooperation and Child Development (NIPCCD) and its regional centres to bring the provisions of CEDAW closer to state-level and government functionaries and NGOs. Some NGOs like 'Sakhi' have been conducting seminars and workshops for promoting awareness about CEDAW amongst women activists and lawyers. However, awareness about CEDAW continues to poor not only amongst the general public but also amongst women groups and lawyers.

Initiatives Undertaken in India

At the national level, the government has given protection in country's Constitution along with providing legislative safeguards under various laws enacted from time to time. The country's Planning Commission has also been giving special attention to women's development and empowerment. In addition, the government has been constituted and appointing Commissions and committees to study and examine the conditions of women in general, and women labour in particular.

Planning Commission

The Planning Commission of India set up the Central Social Welfare Board in 1953 to promote welfare work through voluntary organisations, charitable trusts and philanthropic agencies during the First Five Year Plan (1952-1956) period. The Second Five Year Plan (1956-1960) supported development of *mahila mandals* for grass root work among women. The Third, Fourth and Interim Plans (1961-74) made provision for women's education, pre-natal and child health services, supplementary feeding for children, nursing and expectant mothers. The Fifth Plan (1974-1978) marked a major shift in the approach towards women, from welfare to development. The Sixth Plan (1980-85) accepted women's development as a separate economic agenda. The Multidisciplinary approach with three-pronged thrust on health, education and employment. The Seventh Plan (1985-1990) declared its objective to bring women into the mainstream of national development. The Eight Plan (1992-1997) projected paradigm shift from development to empowerment and promised to ensure flow of benefits to women in the core sectors of education, health and employment. Outlay for women rose from 4 crore in the First Plan to Rs. 2000 crore in the Eighth Plan. The Ninth Plan (1997-2002) stated that empowerment of women was its strategic objective. It accepted the concept of Women's Component Plan to assure at least 30 per cent of funds/benefits from all developmental sectors to flow to women. The Tenth Five Year Plan (2002-2007) suggested specific strategies, policies and programmes for empowerment of women. This was in accordance with The United Nations suggestion that, "to protect the gains of the past and ensure steady progress on indicators of social development and gender equality, and in order to give a fresh impetus to the process of women's empowerment, the Tenth Plan needs to take some bold policy initiatives." These included:

(*a*) Earmarking of funds for women under all major poverty alleviation programmemes and maintenance of gender disaggregated records of implementation of all poverty alleviation programmes;

(*b*) Mandatory registration of all assets provided under government programmes (land, house, animals, production units) in the joint names of husband and wife;

(*c*) Intensified focus on education rights and capacity-building interventions for women in all strategic sectors, including health and reproductive health, agriculture, natural resource management, technology (including information technology) and legal awareness;

(*d*) Revision of regulatory framework to allow women's collectives to access institutional credit, obtain medium-term leases for cultivation on wastelands and common lands, bid for contracts for collection and sale of minor forest produce and other collective activities that will ensure household food security while regenerating the natural resource base.

For the first time during while preparing the Eleventh Five Year Plan (2007-2012) the Planning Commission of India invited several delegations of Women's groups/networks/ think tank of National Alliance of Women's Organisations, Women Power Connect, All India Democratic Women's

Association for tactical sessions to engender the 11th Five Year Plan document. More than 20 women economists/experts from different parts of India provided gender-friendly inputs for various tasks forces on Agriculture, Industry,Law, Environment, Education, Labour, so on and so forth.The Focus is on Empowerment of women.[3]

The state government is also expected to play an important role in empowering women's organisations and citizens groups to monitor enforcement of equal and minimum wages legislation and also to adhere to norms in poverty alleviation programmes.

In first *Human Development Report* (HDR) prepared by the Planning Commission of India the gender disparity across the states indicated a declining graph. The report printed Gender Equity Index (GEI) in which Bihar had the most abysmal record of 0.49, Maharashtra, Orissa, Rajasthan, West Bengal figure in the GEI bracket of 0.6-0.74. The HDR had not seriously taken into account, the declining sex ratio, especially the juvenile sex ratio (0-9 years) while estimating various development indices. It provided a diagrammatic representation of human development in the form of development radars comprising of 8 indicators namely poverty, per capita consumption expenditure, life expectancy at age one, infant mortality rates, intensity of formal education, literacy rates, access to safe drinking water, proportion of households with pucca houses. There was no mention of women development. The central thesis of HDR has been that economic prosperity in terms of high per capita income does not necessarily lead to overall human development. Declining sex ratio in the prosperous states like Punjab, Haryana, Gujarat and Maharashtra prove the point. There is a need to focus more on the impact of budgetary allocations on women's well being and women's development.[4]

The State Government of Maharashtra framed a policy document to bring gender concerns on the social and political agenda, 'Policy for Women in Maharashtra'. As the document declares, the policy was "an attempt to identify immediate steps that the state can take to improve the position of women."

Important features of the policy are:

- Statutory provision for reserving 10 per cent of all income and land at the gram *panchayat* level under the control of women's committee.
- Government allotments and primary memberships of societies to be made in the joint names of husband and wife.
- Amendments in the Hindu Law of Inheritance (1956) for ensuring equal share of the movable and immovable property of the husband.
- Reservation of 30 per cent of government jobs for women.
- Women should constitute 25 per cent of the police force in the State of Maharashtra.
- The state should take steps to re-orient and retain police force and set up women headed police stations in metropolitan cities to safeguard women against violence and atrocities.

HDR, 2002 recommends empowerment of women by better targeting of compulsory elementary education and growth of Medicare in the public domain by public spending. The Report states that focused attention is needed to empower women by:

- Strict enforcement of the legally marriageable age which would, in turn improve their health, give them the time to complete secondary education, correct female-male ratio, delay childbearing tasks till they are ready.
- Punishing female foeticide.
- Avoiding the system of male proxies for elected women and restore true power to women.

- Targeting birth of healthier infants by proper medical measures for women like reducing the number of anaemic.

HDR Maharashtra, 2002 has recommended enhancing nutritional status of women by ensuring security and netting more and more eligible women and children under the Integrated Child Development Scheme (ICDS).

Women and Workplace

Since ages women have always been given an inferior position in the society. Along with inferiority, she had to face the domination, subjugation, and oppression at the hands of men. The roots of oppression can be traced to the essentially patriarchal nature of society where men are in-charge of all societal affairs. They are decision-makers and are solely responsible for framing decisions at several levels of the society such as family, religion, caste, and class. However, over a period of time though the social scenario did change it has not yet reached the goal of equal status for women. The social reform movement and the nationalist movement laid the foundation of the process of significant social change. There were a series of other processes of social change. Industrialisation, modernisation, globalisation created an entirely new set of conditions. Education became very important and subsequently got related with employment.

However this category of women only forms a small minority. If we have to take into consideration a general picture, large number of women does not have access to education, either due to poverty or discriminatory practices. Lack of education and poverty force them to take up employment in the unorganised sector where the exploitation especially on women is very high. Wage discrimination, lack of job security, sexual harassment, absence of proper shelter, basic requirements and medical facilities etc. make women exceedingly vulnerable. As most of them are illiterate or at best semi-literate and with very limited labour union support and limited legal protection, the bargaining power of women is low. They are thus caught in a helpless situation.

The most important change from a feminist viewpoint occurred when women could avail themselves of both education and employment opportunities. They now became educated and financially independent. They developed assertiveness and a sense of individualism. Women no longer remained only homemakers they also became decision takers. In urban areas to some extent professionally women became at par with men in terms of wages and working conditions. Unfortunately, a woman in the organised sector is even now suffering from exploitation in spite of education and sound financial status. Exploitation takes various forms, but the most serious one is sexual molestation at work place. Need for job and absence of alternate job opportunities forces many women to put up with sexual molestation. Apart from being a physical violence, it is also an assault on the dignity and self-respect of women.

Today in the world of work, women's status is subordinate to that of man's as a result of broad sanction such a practice has received over the years. In the general social milieu, the position of woman as worker has generally suffered two types of disadvantages. First, though almost every able-bodied woman is working, either in the home or workplace, she is not being recognized as a worker if she is only housewife. Secondly, whenever she is employed, the status of her employment and remuneration has remained much lower. Another important issue concerns her position in the world of emerging employment scenario where introduction of new technology has been either pushing her out of employment market or bringing her down the ladder of employment opportunities.

In addition, gender bias in employment market is quite rampant either in terms of the type of employment quality or remuneration package. Despite the existence of the Equal Remuneration Act, 1976, it is more often found that women workers are paid less than their male counterparts in many economic activities across different occupations.

With regards to working conditions, they often work in unhygienic conditions: and workplace facilities are rarely provided. Most of them being illiterate and less skilled and consequently, jobs they get are also low paid and manual.

In view of the scattered work place, and home based and piece-rated nature of their employment, they are also highly unorganised. The traditional mind-set of trade unions has virtually ignored the need for their organisation. This lack of organisation has accentuated their so-called 'invisibility' in the main stream employment scenario.

In order to alleviate the situation of women in workplace, both the national government and international bodies, from time to time, have taken up a number of steps and announced a plethora of programmes and schemes to empower women workers. Women empowerment is the key criteria of any programmes to ensure that women get equal rights in workplace and society on the whole.

The labour status can be characterised as the continuum with one segment at the top and the other at the bottom. This includes the set of labour force at the lowest level working not just in subsistence activities but in a variety of commodity production activities. There is another class of labourers who may not be at the bottom but not much above from it, not enjoying much of security or regularity in the employment. This large class is the self employed workers. This leaves a very small segment at the top consisting of the regular salaried working class.

Understanding Unorganised Sector

The term 'unorganised sector' is by the trade unions and those concerned with labour. According to Nirmala Bannerji (1985), "the organized sector usually consists of productive activities with loosely formed groups bound by diverse types of informal working contracts. It includes a section of self employed, wage earners family producers as also household workers". The significance of this definition is that it brings in nature of employment relationship as the main factor that distinguishes organised sector from the unorganised sector. This definition has given three main characteristics of the informal sector: productive activities carried out by loosely formed groups which are bound by informal contracts.[5]

The National Commission on Labour (1966-69) in chapter 20 of its Report, covered the following categories of workers under the heading 'Unorganised Labour' : (*i*) Contract labour including construction workers; (*ii*) Casual labour; (*iii*) Labour employed in small scale industries; (*iv*) Handloom/Power loom sectors; (*v*) Bidi and cigar workers; (*vi*) Employees in shops and commercial establishments; (*vi*) Sweepers and scavengers; (*viii*) workers in tanneries; (*ix*) Tribal labourers; and (*x*) Other unprotected labourers.[6]

Attempts have been made in Indian Labour Organization (ILO) studies to identify and to distinguish the informal sector, which are as follows:

- The small size of operations in terms of capital and labour employed.
- The informal structure and family ownership of the enterprise with practically no functional division of labour and specialisation.
- Use of indigenous and non modern (traditional) technology, which is labour intensive with extremely manual operations, involved in production process.
- Lack of access to state benefits like the benefits of organised capital market, bank finance, foreign technology, foreign exchange concessions, imported raw material, protection from foreign competition and a host of other concessions and incentives which are extended to the enterprise of formal sector by virtue of their having been recognized by the Government.

- Competitive and unprotected product market arising chiefly on account of ease of entry, nature of product produced and its demand and the marketing arrangements which are exploitative.
- Unprotected labour market giving rise to insecure jobs, under employment and depressed wages.[7]

As the unorganised sector is very diverse and encompasses many types of work, it is very difficult to classify it into a specific group as uniform. Although the unorganised sector and organised sector are classified into separate sectors but there is no clear divide between them since often they are interdependent and provide services for each other.

Main Characteristics of the Informal Sector

1. *Ease of entry*: In urban areas, this sector absorbs anyone who wishes to enter. Such sector attracts skilled, unskilled, temporary or permanent workers. There is no need of any formal admission to this sector. For example, rag pickers can enter this field any time. Though the return is not very high, there is surety of job.
2. *Reliance on indigenous resources*: Informal manufacturing sector uses locally, easily and cheaply available materials to produce. Therefore initial cost is very less. Though the overall cost is not much, profit margin is not very high. example cosmetic manufacture like bindis, bangles, rings, rubber bands etc. For other items, the manufacturers also use waste paper, metal scraps, rags etc. Thus promote the efficient use of waste of discarded materials.
3. *Family ownership of enterprise*: Informal sector is so called because it employs mostly family members. Thus labour problem is not much. Further expenditure on labour is saved. This leads to minimum cost of production. Because of this characteristic, the

producers can stay and operate even under unfavourable conditions.

4. *Small-scale of operation*: Established and regular market is not for the informal sector. The manufacturers and those who provide services run their business on small scale i.e. to limited people for example food stalls or street hawkers.
5. *Labour intensive and adapted technology*: The sector absorbs any number of labours since it cannot use modern technology. Even the techniques employed are flexible enough to suit any situation. Normally the workers do not use any machine they work with hands or hand tools.
6. *Skills not formally gained*: Most of the workers learn the craft or skill on the job only. They are not previously trained e.g. in construction industry, workers learn while working.
7. *Market-very unregulated*: Arrangement of sale is not proper as quantity or quality of these products is not under control or regulated. Market is not certain and very unreliable. The manufacturers have to face tough competition with the regular organised sector. Even the prices of the products are not fixed.
8. *Informal Sector is not controlled or officially recognized*: Informal Sector is outside the scope of official regulations governing such matters like getting up of shops or workshops, employers-employees relations, taxation, control of technical skill and product quality. Those who desire to do something but since cannot get chance in organised market are forced to do through informal ways.

Causes of Growth

The various cause of growth of informal sector are as follows:

1. *Rapid urbanisation*: Due to city attractions, as has been observed earlier, a large number of agricultural labour enter the city and find themselves in unemployment situation. Since all cannot get jobs in organised industrial sector, they enter informal sector, and accept any job. They may be wage employed or self-employed. Here any type of worker may be absorbed.
2. *Market consisting of lower and middle class*: Since the middle class is very large there is no shortage of consumers. The informal sector expands very fast.
3. *Abundant supply of labour*: Since migration to city is unrestricted, a number of people enter every day in the city. Not all of them can get job easily or immediately, it takes time to get full-fledged jobs in the formal sectors. Workers accept jobs in the mean time or to fill the gap in the informal sector. There is, therefore, no shortage of supply of labour in this sector e.g. many enter construction work, transport job, home to home delivery or selling, domestic business of selling garments sarees or any consumer items, garages, rag picking (bhangarwala), street hawking, jewellery making etc. Need for finding any source of income encourages people to create jobs.
4. *Creation of employment opportunities*: The informal sector creates abundant employment opportunities in different areas by way of allowing the new comers informally. All types of workers – unskilled, illiterates, inexperienced, skilled, trained men, women and children can be absorbed in this sector without any reservation or control. Therefore, though income is less there is no dearth of job. There is no government intervention or checking system of quality of the products. Further there is no strict wage payment system. The owner of the workshops or production centres maintains informal relations or unwritten code of discipline. Thus employer and employees, seller

and buyers, manufacturer and customers are free to choose each other

5. *Low cost of production*: Due to cheap labour which is easily available and also the involvement of family members in most cases, the initial cost of business is very low. This encourages many entrepreneurs to start business and even with little profit margin in the initial periods, they can manage well.
6. *Informal nature of the sector*: This sector does not need any formal interviews or is particular about specific qualifications among the needy workers. Further the worker is free to choose the employer. The relationship between them is very informal, personal and regulated by need criteria. Law does not control even the payment system; there is no problem of labour confrontation. Workers need not be highly qualified or even educated. With personal contacts jobs can be availed. Most of them are satisfied with their present job. They do not want to switch over to any other job, though most of the entrepreneurs are unaware of the government facilities or programme meant to develop them.

Special Disabilities that the Informal Sector Suffers From

1. *Lack of recognition*: Studies conducted both in Indian and abroad point to special problems which are generally faced by informal sectors. As the enterprises are not officially recognized the entrepreneurs are forced to buy or sell in the unregulated markets where they face a price disadvantage or some sort of semi-permanent relationship based on economic bonded ness. This leads to loss in profits. The entrepreneur being either unregistered or unlicensed, cannot take advantage of any government concessions. Even in the product market, these producers face a severe competition, since they are not organised or united.

They cannot arrange their sale properly. Financiers or those who support them by giving money or raw materials sometimes exploit them and compel them to sell their products to them only.

2. *Lack of facilities*: These informal businessmen cannot effectively utilize any government benefits or any scheme meant for their betterment. Since they are not recognized or registered, or even educated, big entrepreneurs or bureaucrats grab all the benefits provided by the government.
3. *Unauthorised nature of the business*: Most of the activities undertaken in this sector are not formally sanctioned or approved by the government. The producers or sellers face severe space problem. If occupy unauthorised space, they always have to face threatening either from police or municipal officers. Thus lack of approval or recognition from the government side result in severe insecurity among the businessmen in this sector.
4. *Marginal Productivity or Profitability of the sector*: Though number of workers in this sector is very large, the total productivity is very low and return is also very poor. Therefore the standard of workers is very low. Many of those who are employed are below poverty line. Government should support them in order to make them self reliant by providing credit facility and technical know-how.
5. *Types of informal sector employment*: According to studies conducted, informal sector employment is found mostly in manufacturing, commerce and services—where it accounts for nearly 4/5th of the total employment in this sector. And within manufacturing, informal employment is found to be concentrated in food, clothing, footwear and furniture manufacture.
6. *Workers*: Workers are found to be young, predominantly male, fairly literate and belong to backward

and minority communities. They are basically immigrants having coming down to cities from neighborhood states. They are persons hailing from rural areas where they have little or no land to fall back upon for their livelihood. Since most of these immigrants are untrained and unskilled, they cannot find job in the formal sector. Therefore, they're absorbed in the informal sector. Organised sectors can provide high wages but the real costs associated with finding and paying for the accommodation, travel and initial costs have been very high. The informal sector provides job and other facilities either free or at subsidized rates. Thus informal sectors have acted as pull factors to draw the rural migrants to the urban area. In fact, this sector is said to comprise of poor households and workers. The various factors put together engage a substantial percentage of labour force in the informal activities for instance in Calcutta and Mumbai about 50 per cent of the work force is found engaged in this sector.

7. *Potentiality of the informal sector*: There is immense scope for expansion in the informal sector. Since the city grows by leaps and bounds and without any interruption, there is always availability of raw materials like waste etc. and no dearth of customers. For example, in food industries or small products like handkerchiefs, cosmetics, kitchen wares which are generally sold in local trains, in subways or on jobs in this sector. Since migrants continuously flow to the cities and they need jobs very badly there is also no shortage of labour either. Most of the workers are self-employed.

Rapid growth in urban population and its consequences in terms of worsening employment problems, increasing poverty and deteriorating urban environment constitutes a major development challenge facing policy planners and urban authorities in developing countries. With growth rates of urban population having exceeded the employment growth rate in the modern sector of the economy, the structural excess supply of labour resulting from this imbalance has led to the emergence and rapid growth of what is known as the 'urban informal sector'. The huge migration of people into the urban areas for establishing future operations and the consequent population explosion have all said adversely on employment, poverty alleviation and deterioration of urban environment which constitutes a major development challenge facing policy planners and urban authorities in developing countries.

Even though the world has become more and more technology and information technology driven, the informal sector has been an enigma. Heterogeneity of the sector; overbearing influence of the environment in which it operates; inseparability of living and working conditions of the workers, because of the dominance of family workers; and the disadvantages of being informal i.e., segregation and isolation from the formal stream have all been the major factors deterring initiatives to promote and develop informal sector. These are some of the symptoms of economic crisis. On the other hand, developing nations are all pinning their hopes on this sector for future employment generation, to alleviate poverty and they have been exploring alternative solutions to enhance the capacity of this sector to generate additional productive employment. Despite the synchronized global slump, the informal sector is acting as a prime mover in enhancing small business growth and generating employment.

Women who constitute almost 50 per cent of humanity contribute significantly to the country's economy and its social life today. Today they have acquired their own role in the growth and development of an economy. In the past women were not treated as the integral part of the labour force. They entered the labour market after the introduction of machine. Economic condition forced women to seek employment. In modern times they supplement the earnings of the families.

In times of labour shortage they were employed in large numbers but when they demanded for labour contracted they were first to be retrenched. Thus they constituted reserve labour force. They were largely employed in work, which required little or no skill, and their wages were low. By and large their significance was marginal. In the Indian society where transition from traditionalism to modernisms is taking place working of women outside home is being encouraged.

Women in Informal/Unorganised Sector

Urban informal sector consists of small-scale units engaged in the production and distribution of goods and services with the primary objective of generating employment and income for their participants notwithstanding the constraints on capital Ideologically, males are viewed as producers who provide material needs of their women and children, women on the contrary are treated as 'consumers' whose place is in the household and perform socially defined roles of cooking of food and caring of children. The division of work among men and women rather than being arbitrary, is socially defined. Women play multiplicity of roles that far exceeds those of her counterpart. The moment she becomes able, she starts nurturing younger siblings, brings water, collects fuel, carries food to her parents at work, and extends a helping hand to her mother in cleaning and sweeping the house and in cooking. When married she is overburdened with household tasks, child and animal care and farm work and appreciated for her fertility to produce a male child. During childbearing stage, the women reach the top of their productivity and social responsibility and become strong and obedient 'servants'. They prepare and preserve food, provide water and fuel wood, care for the aged and generally knit their family together, young women invariably supports their families, through 12-15 hours remunerative work. Since most of the work performed by women is informal nature, it remains unreported. As there is no wage attached to such work, it does not satisfy the employment criteria and hence remains unaccounted while estimating women's work participation rates.

During the early phase of industrialisation, home based job-work was a typical 'putting out' system in Europe and also in developing and under developing countries like India. This job became very convenient for women. She earned daily wages from her finished product. A micro-level study observed that women are compelled to undertake such irregular jobs due to the low income earned by their counterparts. By such opportunities women not only make a small saving for her but also play the role of provider for her family. Her advantage is to minimize the number of days at work and encourage her subordinates in the family along with growing children to join the earning group for the family.

Nirmala Banerjee, in her study women workers in the unorganised sector in many developing countries demonstrated that there are women workers are disproportionately represented in informal sector occupations. Micro level studies, focussing on women participation in informal sector have further led to several interesting hypotheses:

- Women do not figure as main bread earners.
- They are treated as supplementary workers.
- Women employment is increasing only in such low levels of jobs, which are ignored by men as below their expectations.
- Women participation is not uniform across different age groups. It is high among young girls and older women.

Women workers in informal sector are largely target earners. They are forced by family circumstances to take up work to earn a target income which is usually the gap between consumption requirements of the family and what their male members of the family earn. For large majority of women who are poor, informal sector is the sole source of their livelihood. There is gross underestimation or under-valuation of women employment, as it is hidden and not clearly visible. Employment of women in informal sector received least attention in research in this field. Whatever little evidences are available, however, indicated that women belonging to poor households have little or no education and training.[7]

There are many developing countries already standing out as examples for employment opportunities in informal sector. These are believably small business opportunities, which come in various shapes and sizes, at unexpected times and places. However, in the informal sector, India is unquestionably a world leader. As the workers in developing world countries get more and more pushed into the informal sector area, I strongly believe that countries like India would have more market opportunities and we must cash on it. i.e. generating more self employment opportunities for men as well as women.

A large number of working women in the cities of the developing nations understand the potential of the informal sector. This is so mainly because of the low risk employment opportunities offered by this sector. There are large opportunities in small business retail trading, market vending, ready-to-eat food selling, or household workers and even small job-works conducted from homes. However, some problems still exist as they still have to grapple with a number of common issues like childbearing and child rearing. Family members do not always support working women so they are under tremendous pressure during working hours. A sex-discriminatory legal disadvantage is also a vital issue. In such cases a woman will have to continue her fight for justice and continue to be a part of the economy drive. They are also exposed to social disadvantages, which include inferior education or complete lack of access to formal education, lack of access to resources and skills, and unpaid household tasks. The informal sector which is generally known as holding sector holds rural migrants and unemployed citizens mainly consists of people who are self-employed and provide needful services but in an unorganised and unauthorised manner e.g. street hawker. This sector may cover wide range of activities like retail and wholesale trading, repairing and servicing, casual labour and manufacturing, etc areas like manufacturing, construction transport, trade and services may be considered as informal sectors. Everything with this sector is informal – no formal training, lack of formal credit mechanism, no formal recognition by civic authorities and very often no formal enumeration even in the census.

Problems of Working Women

The profile of women workers highlights the fact of their underestimation and also their concentration in low paid jobs and under presentation in high profile jobs. The working conditions of low-paid employment are equally appalling. As a result, women may be more prone to health hazards and drudgery as compared to their male counterparts. Moreover, skill requirement for performing low-paid jobs is also less. Hence, the prospect for enhancing skill-level of women is also very low.

Besides, majority of women workers are in unorganised sector, which means their job security is conspicuous by its absence. Because of low level of earning and high dependency ratio, their role in different spheres of life is also marginal. The continuation of this situation creates vicious circle which can be broken by strong policy measures and programme designs in which women's participation is prerequisite.

One of the ways in which women's emancipation in economic status and position can take place is through the promotion of informal sector. Informal sector results in income generation and provides economic security to women. The researcher, through this study, has tried to draw strong linkages between the informal sector and economic security for women.

In informal sector a women has to go through various difficulties /problems as she has to manage both fronts (house and business), mostly such women are semi literate, the finance conditions are not good enough to start business. Major problems related to workingwomen are as below:

No training opportunities: To meet the modern technological needs in farming, women should be promoted for such education. This will help the women to develop business skills and understand her status in society, which will help her to be a provider and support her family.

Health problems: Since women are in contact with hazardous chemicals and the like in factories and their working places they are prone to sickness. They also have to work as per working hours and their wages are very low as compared to their male counterpart. Importance for small medical centres in the locality, sanitation, housing, clean drinking water, crèches for their children are some of the hurdles faced by the women.

Motherhood and childcare: All rights of women should be protected including her maternity provisions, which include childcare since such provisions are not reserved for the unorganised sector.

Sexual abuse: Another major problem facing almost 75 percent of the women anywhere are facing sexual harassment at their work place. Women from the lower strata working in the unorganised sector however relate that they are victimized in a very systematic manner. They are the local industries like fish drying, meat packing, mining, etc. The contractor's employ trusted middle women who force young girls to submit to the lust of their contractors and his men. Any refusal will mean their dismissal. In certain situations when the girls are away from home they are physically tortured. This is common among Kerala girls working in the Veraval Port and in Gujarat as well as South Indian girls working in meat packing units.

Access to resources: The corporate image building banks who are product-related and are even customer related may not easily give loans to unskilled women entrepreneurs without the support of guarantors and collaterals. The allocation for women's welfare in the state budgets is also very low.

Problem of choice of techniques: Majority of women in the informal sector work with backward techniques and choice of introducing modern machines may be very expensive for this sector. Women from the informal sector are no doubt vulnerable and easy targets for exploitation compared to their male counterparts. The other issues include gender discrimination in terms to access to resources, skill training, credit and marketing facilities, and job access and job mobility. The answer to these different forms of discrimination and resulting voluntary retirement lies not in asking women to change their beliefs and values, but in strengthening their hands through organising poor women at work in informal sector.[8]

Everything with this sector is informal—no formal training, no formal credit mechanism, no formal recognition by civic authorities and very often no formal enumeration even in the census. A number of schemes set up by governments have managed to reach them only at the periphery. On the contrary, in many countries like India, Bangladesh and the Philippines it is in the NGOs who have been able to make a more tangible impact on solving their problems. Their working conditions may be deplorable, but informal sector workers create their own jobs with very few outside resources. They recycle indigenous material and produce goods for which there is a demand. They also create a huge parallel economy, which is not taken into account in the national production statistics.

The United Nations have chalked out a comprehensive programme by means of various conventions to uplift and develop the status of women in the field of education, politics including the position in social life with the formation of the Commission on Human Rights and the Commission on the Status of Women in 1946 and the adoption of the Universal Declaration of Human Rights in 1948. The United Nations had also undertaken a massive research study to assess the position and status of women across the world. It has been found that in many parts of the world the women have constantly been denied equality in law and also in practice. They are compelled to live under male dominated world and are subjected to variety of discriminations. As a result the United Nations have incorporated a series of treaties and Conventions to achieve the equal legal and political rights of women worldwide.

In the following section we will examine some of the Acts that have been enacted in India to protect labourers in general and women in particular.

The Maternity Benefit Act, 1961

The act is to regulate the employment of women in certain establishments for certain periods before and after the birth of the child and to provide maternity and other benefits. Section 5 of the act gives women the right to payment of maternity benefit. Section 7 gives right in case of death in the course of child birth. Section 8 lays down provisions for medical bonus. Section 9 and 10 provide for leaves in cases of miscarriages or illness. Section 11 of this act lays down provisions for nursing breaks. Every women is entitled to this benefit if she has worked in the establishment for a period not less than eighty days of the twelve months immediately preceding the date of her expected delivery and the maximum period for which any woman shall be entitled to maternity benefit shall be twelve weeks of which maximum six weeks shall precede the date of her expected delivery . In the sampled construction site no such provisions were observed to be complied with by the owners. In this construction work whenever the women are pregnant they are removed from work. They are informed to join after the delivery. No maternity benefit is provided. Since there is no trade union the matter is never looked into by any organization.

The Equal Remuneration Act, 1976

The Act provides for equal remuneration to men and women and protects the interest of women at workplace. But on the construction site unequal remuneration was paid on the basis of sex and so therefore this act is not practiced by the owners of the sampled construction site.

India has a considerable number of labour laws for protecting the interest of workers. However most of the laws are applicable to workers in the organised sector that constituted little more than eight per cent of the total workforce in 1993–94. However, there are two Acts which have special relevance to women labours, namely, Equal Remuneration Act, 1976 and Maternity Benefit Act, 1961. Both the acts provide for safeguards to women labourers their equal wages and maternity benefits.

The women workers of the sampled site were ignorant about their rights enshrined in various labour laws made by the government from time to time. And this is the primary reason that they are exploited by the owner/*mukadams*.

The Contract Labour (Regulation and Abolition) Act, 1970

The main objective of this legislation is to take care of variety of unfair practices of the intermediaries and to provide required facilities to the contract workers in view of the peculiar circumstances in which they work. Sections 16, 17, 18 and 19 of the act fix obligations on employers to provide welfare and health facilities like the canteen, rest rooms, first aid facilities etc.

The Bonded Labour System (Abolition) Act, 1976

The WCT (Works Contract Act) provides for the abolition of the system with a view of preventing the economic and physical exploitation of the weaker sections of the society. Section 2 of the act prohibits any money taken or given as advance in cash or kind as consideration of the work being done by him or her. What does this mean but surprisingly this provision of the Act is openly floated both by the workers as well as the employers at the construction site, Bhandup west.

The Workmen Compensation Act, 1923

This Act provides for a quicker and cheaper disposal of disputes relating to compensation in respect of any injury occurred during employment. However if there is some serious injury like fractures of the hand and feet, the employees do not give any compensation to these workers according to the provisions of the act. Some money though is given to them at times but just on humanitarian grounds or as debt which is later on deducted from the payment paid to the worker.

The Employees' State Insurance Act, 1948

The objective of the Act is to introduce an integrated system of health, maternity and accident insurance providing for certain benefits. These benefits are secured by the financial contributions to the scheme both by the employers and the workers. The Act provides for six types of benefits to which the insured person and his dependents are entitled. These benefits relate to sickness, maternity, disablement, dependents, medical and funeral. In the sampled site, the act was not being complied with the owners and there were no provisions for workers insurance and the contribution from them and their employers.

The Employer's Provident Fund and Miscellaneous Provisions Act, 1952

On inquiries, it was found that the women workers in the area were not aware of the ESI act. The lack of awareness among the female workers and many of the male workers is one of the major reasons that these workers have little motivation towards such type of social security legislations. However the owner and the male workers were unaware about the Employees Provident Fund and Miscellaneous Provisions Act 1952. According to the owner this act cannot be implemented in true spirit as the labourers many a time change their work site and thereby change their owner. So the owner is of the view that the government should give service cards to the workers of the construction site to enable them to pay regular contribution wherever they go.

The Payment of Bonus Act, 1965

According to Section 8 of this act every worker is entitled to some bonus to be paid by his employee, provide the worker has worked in the establishment of more than thirty working days in a year. However on the sampled construction site, no such arrangement was observed to have been done by its owners and so they do not comply with the provisions of the bonus act as such.

There are laws which are there to protect women's right and to treat her as human being. In actual practice these laws do not benefit the women in practical terms due to lack of awareness, poverty, and illiteracy. Also enforcement of such laws are rarely used unless media, NGO's intervention is there.

In informal sector the basic human rights violation can be seen such as discrimination in wage on basis of gender, even though the work content is same or important as what men perform. The women are treated as additional help where the couple can earn additional income. In informal sector lack of sanitation, no washroom, no space for changing dress are very common factor as violation of human rights. If the employers are providing such facilities in certain case, these are temporary in nature and are unsafe and unhygienic. One of the major areas of concern in informal sector is crèche. As there are no crèche provided by employer or municipal corporation the women have to either carry the child to their workplace on their back or make temporary cloth cradle at the work site, which is dangerous and unsafe for the child and mother.

REFERENCES

1. Gender Role Beliefs and Stress in Working Women, *Urdhva Mula* , Vol. 1, No. 1, November 2002, pp. 63-65.
2. Saksena, A., *Implementation of the Convention on the Elimination of Discrimination Against Women(CEDAW) in India with Reference to Women Workers*, Report submitted to the Department of Civics and Politics, University of Mumbai under the University Grants Commssion's Department Special Assistance Programme, 2003.
3. Patel, Vibhuti, *Feminist Jurisprudence-Contemporary Concerns*, Majlis, Mumbai, 2002.
4. *Op.cit.*
5. Banerjee, Nirmala, *Why They Get A Worse Deal*, Siddhi Publishers, Hyderabad, 1989.
6. Murty, S., *Women and Employment*, RBSA Publisher, Jaipur, 2001.
7. Bannerjee, Nirmala, *Women Workers in the Unorganized Sector*, Sangam Books, Hyderabad, India,(1985).
8. ILO, *Employment, Income, Equality: A Strategy For Increasing Productivity Employment In Kenya*, ILO, Geneva, 1972.

Construction Industry and Condition of Work

Construction industry is the second largest employer in India, next only to agriculture. Of the estimated total employment of about 36.9 crore in the unorganised sector, 3 crore are found in construction industry alone. Construction industry is also one of the largest industries absorbing maximum number of migrant labour force. Some of the unique features of construction industry are:

- It's the only industry where the product is static whereas the production process is dynamic.
- Although construction activity requires high precision skills except for a mini scale formally trained cadre the major dependence is on indigenous skills or the unskilled labour force, learning on the job.
- The relationship between the employer and the employee is very complex supposed to be regulated by the so called contracts. However the principal employer remains an invisible and unaccountable entity.
- In the process of development government investment large amount in construction activity, but exclusive

and comprehensive legislation to protect labour rights of the construction workers is yet to materialize.

- There is a preference for employing labour force derived from the seasonal rural migrants. Most of the time there is conscious recruitment of such labour force through contracts and petty contractors.
- The construction activity is multilayered happening in phases resulting short duration jobs.
- Except in the repair and maintenance aspect the work force stay at the work place itself thus depending on the employer for their survival.
- It is also one of the most hazardous industries.[1]

Employment in construction is usually interrupted with periods of unemployment of varying duration mainly due to fluctuating requirements of labour force on each work site. The nature of work is such that there are no holidays. Interview reveals that the female workers do not get minimum wage. Though skilled workers secure jobs directly from employers, unskilled workers by and large, are engaged through intermediaries who introduce the workers to contractors on a commission basis. The payment of wages is given through the intermediaries who usually enroll workers by offering loans. These loans are then recovered by manipulating the wages of workers, with the result that the workers hardly get out of the clutches of the intermediaries, since workers are generally recruited on contract basis, failing to achieve the required quantum of work results in either deduction or uncompensated overtime work. In return for providing job, intermediaries often collect commission from each worker at a fixed rate for each working day. Among these, women workers are more vulnerable to various types of exploitation. These construction workers may or may not be migrant workers but they have maximum mobility because of the nature of their occupation. They are always on move from one work-site to another after the construction work at a site is over. These workers also migrate from backward/ small industrial, urban and commercial centre to develop and big industrial, urban and commercial centre. The development of a particular urban centre also depends on its political importance. Political importance boosts up industrial, infrastructure development process and this in turn boosts up construction works. Though they are part and parcel of the large streams of workers, their problems and woes are, in fact, continuation of the problems and woes faced by the workers of other sectors.[2]

Construction works require various kinds of skilled and unskilled workers like *coolies* (these workers are used to pass material from one place to another without help of any machine or equipement. At the most they use *ghamalas* to carry bricks, cement etc.*)*, *beldars* (workers who mix cement and water to form the correct paste), *rajmistris* (these workers are considered to be skilled workers who actually do the plastering or joining of bricks in line with cement), painters (workers who only do the painting job), *badhais* (these are workers who do skilled work of wood/flooring related job), plumber (any job where water connection and pipe fitting is to be done) etc. Women are mostly used as helpers in various jobs and as *coolies.*These workers are spread across the width and length of the country; however, they are drawn in large numbers, through pull and push factors to the emerging and flourishing industrial and urban centers. So, these centers have huge concentration of construction workers. Most of the workers in this sector are employed on a casual basis. Unstable employment, earnings and shifting of work places are the basic characteristics of work for construction workers.

Construction workers fall in the category of unorganised sector. Though this predicament is not exclusive to them, however, highly disorganised and fragmented state hamper their bargaining power and fight against injustice. Neither their job nor their work at a particular site is permanent or of a perennial nature. When construction starts at any place, these workers are hired on daily or monthly or may be on contract basis. The duration and security of their employment depend upon the kind of employment they enter into. It may last for days, for weeks, for months and may be, if they are fortunate, for a year or so. After that they need to look for another site and employment. So, neither the work site is fixed nor the employment is permanent. May be they have their own sources and network and channel of information and employment, but this doesn't lessen their problems and difficulties. This predicament creates lot of hassles for them and provides sufficient grounds for their exploitation by the employers.

Being part of unorganised sector of labourers and not being part of the unionisation process they are unable to find in bargaining for fair wages; illiteracy and ignorance regarding laws aggravates the problems. They are not paid minimum wages; even the agreed wages are not paid in time.[3] Even after the construction work is over, substantial due remains with the builders or the contractors, who are always on the look for devouring these due wages. Moreover, their working time and hours are not well regulated. They do not get overtime rates for excess work. They work under very hazardous conditions. The working conditions and the facilities provided at the sites are far from satisfactory. Safety conditions and measurers are hardly met. It is not uncommon to see them working in precarious conditions, at great height without any safety mechanisms in place. In case of accident, there is, in general, no provision for financial and medical aid. It is up to the workers themselves to arrange for the treatment. There is no scheme like ESI coverage for them. In the extreme cases like death, no body owns the responsibility. Apart from these, there is no recreational facilities, no availability of drinking water, toilets, canteens etc. In big cities, like Delhi, they face another big problem of commuting from one place to other. They have to commute on their own if the construction workers are from local area. Travelling from the place of living to the work site and then back to the living place eat much into their time, money and energy. The commutation is not even smooth. Therefore they have no much of leisure to spend with family, and less of money and energy to cater the needs of family members.[4]

Due to constant movement in construction business the workers mainly live a nomadic life. They move along with the builders or with the contractor. This is also due to the fact that majority of the workers have migrated from outside Mumbai and do not have their own house to live. Hence dependency on contractor or builder is high. The employers provide place for temporary house to these workers. This result in no ration cards for these workers and also no voting identity card, this effect their status in society. Also they are deprived from basic right to vote. The benefits provided by the government for poor in terms of, rice, sugar, wheat, kerosene etc at subsidised rate are also not available to these workers.

The Government of India has, apart from seeking to implement the laws mentioned in the earlier chapter, enacted, over the years a number of Acts to give special protection to this vulnerable group of workers. It is to this aspect that we will turn our attention.

Building and Other Construction Workers (Regulation of Employment and Working Conditions) Act, 1996

The above Law aims to provide for regulation of employment & conditions of service of the building and other construction workers as also their safety, health and welfare measures in every establishment which employs or employed during the preceding year ten or more workers. The exception made is only in respect of residential houses for own purpose constructed with a cost not exceeding Rs. 10 lakh and such other activities to which the provisions of Factories Act, 1948 and Mines Act, 1952 apply. Some of the other main provisions of the Main Act are given below:

1. Provision for an Advisory Committee at the Central and the State levels with the function to advise the Governments concerned on such matters arising out of the administration of the Act as may be referred to it.
2. Provision for registration of each establishment within a period of sixty days from the commencement of work to ensure that there are no malpractices and to discourage non-compliance of law by circumventing.
3. Provision for registration of building workers as beneficiaries under this Act.
4. Provision for constitution a Building and Other Construction Workers' Welfare Board by every State Government to exercise the powers conferred on, and perform the functions assigned to it, under the Act.
5. Provision for immediate assistance in case of accidents, old age pension, loans for construction of house, premia for group insurance, financial assistance for education, to meet medical expenses, maternity benefits etc.
6. Provision for health and safety measures for the construction workers in conformity with ILO convention No.167 concerning safety and health in construction revising the Safety Provisions (Building) Convention, 1937. For this purpose comprehensive Central Rules i.e. Building and other Construction Workers (Regulation of Service and Conditions of Service) Central Rules, 1998 have been notified by the Central Government.
7. Provision for constitution of safety committees in every establishment employing 500 or more workers with equal representation from workers and employers in addition to appointment of safety officers qualified in the field.

8. Provision for Penalties of fine and imprisonment for violation and contravention of the Act.

To raise the Funds for provision of various welfare measures, the Main Act provides for constitution of Welfare Boards. The major source of the Funds shall be collection of cess at rates not exceeding 2 per cent of the cost of construction incurred by an employer. The collection of funds and administration of the Welfare Boards would be the responsibility of concerned State Governments.[5]

The Building and Other Construction Workers' Welfare Cess Act, 1996 (28 of 1996)

The Key purpose of this Act is to argument the resources of the Building and Other Construction Workers' Welfare Boards constituted under the Building and Other Construction Workers (Regulation of Employment and Conditions of Service) Act,1996. It extends to the whole of India and came in to force on the November 3, 1995.

Under the Act 1 per cent cess shall be collected from every employer where the cost of construction is more than Rs. 10 lakhs. The proceeds of the cess so collected shall be paid by the local authority or the State Government collecting the cess to the Board after deducting the cost of collection of such cess not exceeding 1 per cent of the amount collected.

Further, the Central Government may, by notification in the Official Gazette, exempt any employer or class of employers in a State from the payment of cess payable under this Act where such cess is already levied and payable under any corresponding law in force in that State.

Responsibility for enforcement of the Act primarily lies with the State Governments/UTs.[6]

Having seen the condition of construction workers in general and the Laws enacted by the Government of India we will now turn our attention to the women workers in the construction industry.

General Conditions of Female Construction Workers

In construction industry women are more vulnerable for low-skilled, low paying jobs engaged only in unskilled occupation like helpers or coolies. Also with the introduction of new machineries there will be reduction in employment opportunities particularly for women since they are only engaged in unskilled work.

A large number of women workers 1.27 per cent of all women workers (as compared to 4.17 per cent of all male) are employed in the construction industry. Among them more than 98 per cent are casual workers where as the proportion of casual workers among women workers in all industries together is far less about 75 per cent With increasing mechanization it is the women casual workers who are the first victims of displacement in the nearly all construction operations. Their labour in operations in which they have been traditionally deployed, soil digging and carrying, carrying inputs in concrete mixing and placing concrete curing and brick carrying is going to be eliminated completely soon. As it is estimated that overall deployment of labour will become 1/50th to 1/5th of the earlier numbers obviously women will be increasingly eliminated from construction sites.[7]

It is universally observed that in a society which is characterized by gender segregation and social stratification certain sections unfortunately occupy a subordinate position. Indian constitution guarantees democracy and confers the right of equality to all strata. But the reality is that this guarantee and right of equality have not reached many lower sections of society. It is those people who struggle, are impoverished, alienated and concerned with basics for survival. The case of women construction workers is evidence to the fact that despite the guaranteed constitutional rights their struggle for equality and survival continues. It is disheartening to note that women construction workers as a part of unorganized work force remain the most exploited ones even after six decades of independence. Women workers at construction site have to face various problems and while commuting gets compounded and multiplied. More so if they are pregnant or have young children. There is no system at all to take care of these children at work site. And they just cannot take leave out of work during this period least they would face extreme financial problems. Then, living conditions are no way better than the working conditions. It will not be entirely wrong to say that the situation is still worse. They are destined to live in slums where one does not get proper civic amenities. The surroundings are totally unhygienic. There are no proper facilities for drainage, toilet, potable water, electricity, recreation etc. There are no local medical facilities, hospital, school and fair price shop. They need to struggle quite a lot to get ration cards, they hardly avail the facility of banking services, for postal services they have to travel to far away localities. For all these reasons, it is very difficult for them to maintain healthy community life. Most of the time construction workers are forced to live nearby or at the work site. At these sites living conditions/lack of civic and other facilities are even more appalling.[8]

The women in the construction industry comprised mostly of migrants accompanying their spouses or relatives. Majority of these women take up work along with their male counterparts. However there are also women accompanying their spouses and staying on the sites but not taking up any work. There is the third category of women coming in the open labour market independently seeking job.

Women construction workers are prone to three types of exploitation which can be properly described in the feminist triple burden theoretical perspective.

1. They have to prove themselves as workers contributing to the productivity of the construction industry as human resource. Almost 8 to 10 hours of the day they live the life of a labourer putting in work equal to that of men.

2. The major part of their lives is taken up by their biological role of reproductivity. Child bearing and rearing becomes the mainstay of their life. In a patriarchic society these roles have to be effectively played without any formal support system or accessible health services. Lack of improper medical facilities, poverty and improper hygienic conditions, women have delivery done at their temporary shelter provided by builder. Without any rest they have to go back to work immediately after delivery. This makes them vulnerable to various illness.

3. They are solely responsible to set up home with meager resources or no resources and prove themselves a wives, homemaker and mothers. They have to bear the secondary treatment due to the patriarchic culture of the society. They are they forced to tolerate and bear the drudgery and menial tasks delegated to them at work place and home and in the society due to poverty, illiteracy. Women remain in the domain of menial unskilled category throughout their life. In spite of putting in equal hard work they are paid less than men or paid just subsistence allowance. The invisible glass ceiling exists here in more blatant form. The construction industry, depending on the traditional skill work is divided on the basis of gender which excludes women totally from the skill formation and skill up gradation process. The aspect leads to deprivation from opportunities of upward mobility.

As mentioned earlier, women come into the industry as the migrant workforce and live on the construction site itself. Once the makeshift shelter is built it is the responsibility of the women to set up home. Invariably, they suffer the most. Majority of the sites do not have basic amenities like toilets, potable adequate water or electricity. Women are forced to adopt unnatural lifestyle with no privacy or safety at the sites.

Even the toilet timings have to be in the middle of the night. There is no enclosure even for bathing or changing clothes. Thus they crave for seemingly simple needs like a latch on inside of the door of their hut, so that they can bolt it and sleep peacefully. Women run kitchens ingeniously without storage facility for edible items, no kerosene or traditional fuel and sometimes no money to buy food.[9]

The worst burden comes in the form of total negligence to their physical health mostly reproductive health. They marry early and survive without any government health coverage. They are forced into delivering babies at home in absolute unhygienic conditions with the help of their neighbours due to poverty and lack of awareness of government hospitals. Their children remain out of the purview of the immunizations campaigns. They are exploited by the employee, contractors and also many times bear sexual harassment and exploitation at work place. They also many times face violence at the hands of their spouses. The burdens are heavy and there are no visible respites. Against this bleak backdrop it is imperative to talk about different ways which will enable and embolden women to seek redress to their complaints, to seek justice in their working life, to seek safer and healthier life and last but not the least to seek a portion of the sky below which women can breathe feely and enjoy sheer joy existence.[10]

In the next chapter we will be highlighting the problems of women in construction industry in Bhandup area. The stress is on identifying the areas where human rights violation is occurring, and inability of government to enforce the laws protecting the rights of Women workers.

REFERENCES

1. ILO-WEP, *Informal Sector and Urban Employment: A Review of Activities in the Urban Informal Sector, International Labour Office, Geneva*, 1990.
2. *Ibid.*

3. Papola T. S., *Urban Informal Sector in Developing Economy*, Vikas Publications, New Delhi, 1981.
4. Dak, T. M., *Women and Work in Indian Society*, Discovery Publishing House, Delhi, 1988.
5. http://labour.nic.in/dglw/building_works.html
6. *Ibid*.
7. Chauhan, P., *Women Labour in India*, V.V. Giri National Labour Institute, Noida, 2007.
8. Muthuraja, C, *Women Folk in Indian Agriculture : An Analysis Of Their Participation And Contribution*, Intelectual Publishing House, New Delhi, 1997.
9. Sethuraman, S. V., *The Urban Informal Sector in Developing Countries ; Employment Poverty and Environment*, International Labour Organisation, Geneva, 1981.
10. Thara Bhai, L., *Women's Studies in India*, APH Publishing Corporation, New Delhi, 2000.

Women in Construction Industry

Case Study

In this chapter we will be examining the status of women construction workers on the basis of an empirical study carried out in Bhandup, a suburb in Mumbai. While no generalisation for the entire industry can be made on the basis of this study it will surely give indicators of the kind of problems construction workers face.

Area Profile of Bhandup

Bhandup is a place located in Mumbai, situated in the State of Maharashtra in India. It is well connected by central railway and roadway. Railway divides Bhandup in two part i.e. Bhandup East and West. As can be seen in the map (*see on next page*) it is well connected by Lal Bahadur Shastri Marg in West and Eastern express highway in East.

As defined by the Municipal Corporation of Greater Mumbai, Bhandup falls within the S-ward. In the last twenty years, the population of Bhandup has risen exponentially. Census 2001 shows population of Bhandup as 691,227 i.e., 21 per cent increase from 1991 census.[3]

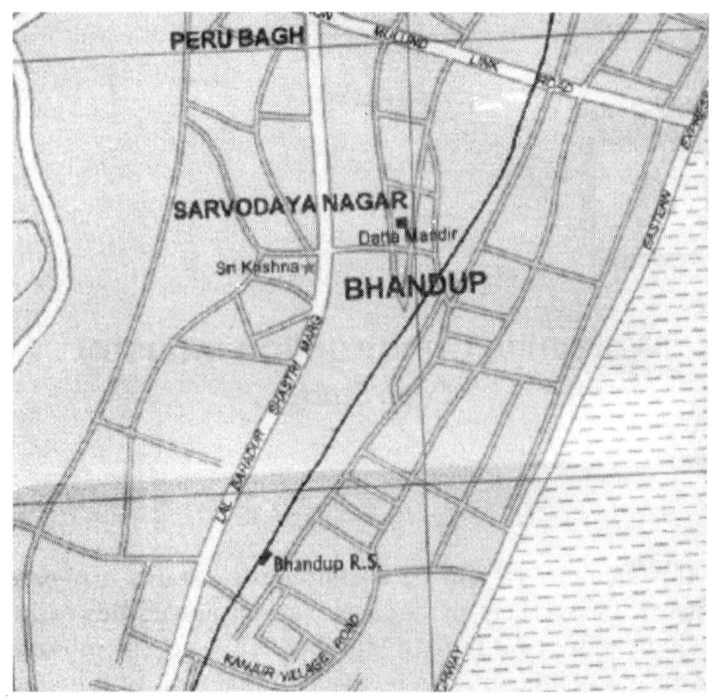

Source: http://en.wikipedia.org/wiki/Bhandup (accessed on May 16, 2009)

Large per cent of the people residing in Bhandup are natives of Maharashtra; in the last couple of decades there has been an influx of non Maharashtrian people. Last decade has seen tremendous growth in Bhandup area. This being centrally located in Mumbai and near Thane many people wanted to have houses here, due to low budget flats as compared to other areas in Mumbai, easy access to schools, colleges, hospitals and shopping malls which have come up in last decade. Along with this major industries started to shift out of Mumbai which resulted in availability of vacant land. This was grabbed by big builders to convert industrial land to residential complex. All this led to increase in construction activities where labour force was required in large number in this Bhandup area. Mostly migrant workers are available at cheaper rate. This has made the researcher to highlight the plight of women worker in construction industry.

Women Construction Workers in Bhandup

The present chapter presents comprehensive information about the social economic life of the women workers at Bhandup west. This chapter covers aspects relating to their education, age, marital status, caste, religion, state of domicile and the type of work they perform on the construction site apart from details about their family, number of children,' number of school going children, number of married children etc. It also takes into account the details relating to the economic aspects of these workers like the income of their family, property, expenditure debt etc. The women workers in the construction industry are mainly engaged in unskilled work. They engaged themselves in carrying bricks or cement or earth on a wheelbarrow or in a basket on their head. They clean gravel by throwing it on a large sieve. Women also break bricks into small pieces. This work is mainly done by the older women as it is less strenuous.

To understand the position of women in construction industry it is necessary to go through the status of women in a given society, which cannot be assessed in isolation from the social framework in which they live. Women's status is closely related with the social structure, religion, family, cultural norms and value systems. All these are important determinants of her position and behavior patterns in society as human being.

The researcher has surveyed Neptune society, Bhandup where researcher has interviewed 30 women construction worker working at the construction site. On the basis of data collected the researcher has put forward the following observation and analysis.

Age and marital status: An analysis of the data collected revealed that more than 90 per cent women worker at the construction site were of less than 45 years age; further breakup shows that below 20 years constituted 13 per cent out of the people interviewed and of these 60 per cent were unmarried and were coming along with their brother or mother. The data also showed that total women workers 86 per cent were married. Whereas 2 per cent were either divorced or widows. It was noticed that the widows and divorced were little elderly and came for work along with the families of their sons. On the other hand, the unmarried women workers came to the sites mainly along with their brothers.

Table 4.1 : Distribution of respondents by their age and marital status

Age	Freq-uency	Percen-tage	Marital status	Freq-uency	Percen-tage
Below 20 years	4	13.33	Unmarried	2	6.66
20-35 years	14	46.66	Married	26	86.66
36-45 years	10	33.33	Divorced/Widows	02	6.66
46 and above	02	6.66			
Total	**30**	**100**		**30**	**100**

Religion and caste: It is observed that the maximum workforce in the construction industry comes from the lower castes of the society. Caste wise there were zero women worker from higher caste. But total 75 per cent were schedule caste. Also 80 per cent were Hindu's and 16.66 per cent were Muslim. The women from schedule castes and the backward castes form the major chunk of the labour force at the construction site.

Educational background: The level of education of the sample indicated that (83.0%) of the women workers in the sampled site were illiterate. There were just 26 per cent women workers who had acquired some formal school education. There was not even a single woman in this sample who had passed tenth standard. Reason cited were that of

Table 4.2 : Distribution of respondents according to their religion and caste

Age	Freq-uency	Percen-tage	Caste Only for Hindu	Freq-uency	Percen-tage
Hinduism	24	80	High caste	0	0
Christians	01	3.33	S.C	18	75.00
Muslims	05	16.66	S.T	02	8.33
			O.B.C	04	16.66
Total	**30**	**100**	**Total**	**24**	**100**

poverty and nomadic life. But the survey has also brought some positive side that even though the sample is semi literate, they are having positive approach towards education and desire that their children should not continue the same work what they are doing and so they want their children to be educated and as a result the researcher found that majority of the children of school going age are attending the nearby municipal schools and these women are also taking interest in their children's education. Mothers of young children whose children are not of school going age are also eager to send their children to school and it has been observed by the researcher that there has been no discrimination on the basis of sex.

Area from where respondents have migrated: Survey reveals that maximum women workers have migrated from South Indian states like Karnataka, Tamil Nadu, Andhra Pradesh and only a few belonged to north eastern states like Assam and W. Bengal. There were a few local women construction worker who were from Maharashtra and came from nearby slums to work at the construction site on day to day basis. The state wise analysis of the data showed that 40 per cent of the women worker in the sample were from Karnataka, 23.33 per cent of the women workers were from Tamil Nadu, 16.66 per cent of the women were from Andhra Pradesh, 3.33 per cent of the women from Orissa, 6.66 per cent of the women from West Bengal and the remaining 10.00 per cent of the women were from Maharashtra (the native state).

Table 4.3 : Distribution of respondents according to the state of domicile

Sl. No.	State	Number of Respondent	Percentage
1.	Karnataka	12	40.00
2.	Tamil Nadu	7	23.33
3.	Andhra Pradesh	5	16.66
4.	Orissa	1	3.33
5.	West Bengal	2	6.66
6.	Maharashtra	3	10.00
7.	**Total**	**30**	**100**

Nature of work: The women workers in the construction industry are mainly engaged in unskilled work. An analysis of the sampled women workers of the site also revealed that they are engaged in unskilled work and mostly work as helpers to their male counterparts on the site. They engaged themselves in carrying bricks or cement or earth on a wheelbarrow or in a basket on their head. They clean gravel by throwing it on a large sieve. Women also break bricks into small pieces. This work is mainly done by the older women as it is less strenuous. Women also mix motor. Sometimes instead of climbing up a ladder to take bricks to the first floor, the woman throws up the bricks one by one by and the mason catches them.

No safety equipments provided by the builder. Working hours are not fixed. Personal protective equipment like handgloves, helmet, glass for eyes etc, are not provided. If injured (minor) no medical facilities is provided, in fact they are told not to come till fit to work.

Family background: The analysis showed that over 80 per cent families of the women worker in the site were nuclear family mainly comprising of the husband and their children. It was because these workers migrate with their husbands and children and leave their elderly parents to look after their houses at the native places. While migrating, only the earning members of the families and the small children are preferred to be taken along. However in some cases i.e.15 per cent families have sister, younger brother who is not married or mother along with them at the site.

The employment status of husbands on the construction women workers reveal that majority (96.6 per cent) of the husbands of these women are earning at the construction site along with their wives. However 3.4 per cent husbands are dependent on their wives as they suffer from same illness/ diseases.

Though the Human Rights Act provides that if more than 30 women are employed, crèche has to be provided by employers no such facility is provided to the women worker. Wages also are not given as per the law (Minimum Wage Act) Discrimination on basis of gender is observed.

Size of the family: The data showed that 84.55 per cent of the families of the women worker in the area of this study had four to five members in their family and 15.45 per cent of the families of women workers had 2-3 members in the family. 10.2 per cent respondents had 2 children while 21.12 per cent respondents had 3 children and 8.68 per cent respondents had no children. It was surprising to notice that none of the children of the respondents were left at the native place or anywhere else.

The data revealed that vast majority of 88.79 per cent of these women respondents, none of their children were employed, as majority of the children were young. The children of 11.2 per cent respondents were employed with all boys in nearby areas as mechanics, cleaner or as a helping hand at a grocer's shop.

The data revealed that majority (65.12%) number of children of these workers attended nearby municipality school. These children are able to do their schooling as the respondents have been staying at the same construction site for the last 4-5 years as the builder has provided them with temporary houses. As the importance of education is slowly realised by the respondents they are now more particular and serious in sending their children to school without being based on gender. 10.88 per cent of respondents whose children are young and are not of school going age are also very eager to send their children to school. 16.75 per cent of the children of the respondents are school dropouts and out of which 11.35 per cent have started working to assist their family and 7.25 per cent of the girls who are dropouts have got married.

Family income: With regard to the income of women for the whole year (normally they worked for at least 300 days in the year) it was found that 72.44 per cent families were able to earn more than Rs 24,000 annually as the daily wages are Rs. 80 per day for a women worker. As in most of the cases, husbands also work along with their wife and are paid more than their wife, they get higher wages and so their annual wages were more than that of their wives and on an average they earned more than Rs. 30,000 to 35,000. So the total income per pair annually is at least Rs. 55,000 to 65,000. Here also the researcher came to a conclusion that there has been discrimination of wages on the basis of sex which is wide-spread in our country since ages.

Amount of debt and source of borrowings: An analysis revealed than more than 3/4th of (74.5%) the families of these women were under some debt. 50.24 per cent families had an amount of debt less than Rs. 15,000. There were around 14.26 per cent families whose debt was between Rs. 20,000 to Rs. 25,000 and 10. per cent families whose debt was between Rs. 30,000 and 32,000. The data showed that the money was borrowed to meet medical expenses, buy electronic goods, and repay the debt borrowed from the landlord at their native places. However 26.5 per cent families had no debt on them as they never had any dependents to look after.

Reasons for migration from native place to the present destination: The main reasons of migration are poverty, heavy borrowings, and irregular availability of work, irregular wages, and fewer wages. The decision to shift from native place to certain other place is in fact a difficult one. It was found that the sources of encouragement were mainly the family friends. These people encouraged women to migrate by furnishing them with information regarding the prospects of employment, arrangements of stay, and socio-economic variables associated with the work. Majority of them were motivated by their husbands who themselves work at these sites. Very few women have taken the decision of joining the construction site themselves. These women constitute mainly the widows or the divorced women who had earlier accompanied their husbands.

Reasons for joining construction industry: One of the main reasons for joining the construction industry was low skill required for job and especially for women where they were required as helpers and for coolie type work. Also without any skills the family was getting extra income. Nearly three fourth (75.36%) of women stated that the main reason for their joining this industry was that they could work with their husband and also can live in the accommodation provided to them free of cost at the construction site itself. Nearly one fourth (24.60) women workers were of the view that since either their parents or the parents-in-law had been in this job, therefore it was natural for them to adopt their families traditional work. Many workers (21.46%) said that since they do not possess skills for other type of jobs, so the best job for them is to work in the construction industry along with their husbands. Many women workers (17.32%) mentioned that that they can borrow some money as advance from the *mukadams* without interest in times of emergency like sickness or for going to their native place. Better wages as compared to what they were getting in their village was also a reason for joining this industry was however stated by a small proportion of 10.32 per cent women workers.

Family life of women workers: The women workers at the construction site have a dual role; while at the work site, they help their husbands or male counterparts. This includes laborious job without any skills required. After going back to the dwellings they have to devote another 3-4 hours per day for housework. They have to take care of the children, cook food, wash clothes, clean utensils, fetch water from bore well, vegetables and grocery from the nearby markets. Most of the husbands sit idle consuming alcohol or resting. Very less help is expected of them. The survey revealed that nearly 66.1 per cent women workers performed all the household chores by themselves, while 33.9 per cent got help from their family members like husbands, daughter, son, mother-in-law, sister-in-law etc. 10.98 per cent husbands helped their wives while 14.88 per cent got assistance from their daughters. 2.19 per cent women were being helped by their sons and while 5.95 per cent of them were being helped by either their mother-in-law or sister-in-law. Men folk look at their women with suspicion. They subject them to all kinds of enquiries to know the reasons for their coming late from the workplace. The climate at the workplace is not congenial either. They have no security of jobs and no facilities like crèches at their workplace to take care of children. They are required to leave them at home to be taken care of by the older children. Working women are required to work at both fronts - Work and Home. This data was collected through the interview where respondents were asked direct questions regarding their wages and time spent in house doing household chores everyday. All this adds up to the stress and tension that women face on a day to day basis.

Social life and habits of husbands: Women workers were asked about the social life of their husbands. In many cases, the husband's indulged in habits like drinking, gambling and lottery, thereby increasing their burden all the more.

It was found that many husbands take alcohol every day before they go to sleep and some time indulge in wife beating. They feel exhausted after the long hours of work and become easy prey to alcohol. 56.7 per cent husbands drank daily, while 24.86 per cent drank twice or thrice a week, while 18.43 per cent husbands were never addicted to drinking.

Majority of these husbands i.e. 94.13 per cent smoke beedies or cigarettes. Many of them are indulged in purchasing lottery or gambling and playing cards as they have no organised systems of recreational facilities for them. Many of them consume non-vegetarian food and these habits of the husbands are monetarily very expensive and it is possibly one of the reasons that these workers are not able to save money and therefore remain under debt.

Participation in decision making process in the family: Participation in the decision making process of a family is an indicator of the power and control over the affairs of that family. The data reflected that there were only 17.31 per cent women workers who took decisions themselves. These women were either divorced, widowed or whose husbands were addicted to alcohol, lottery or gambling. The findings confirm the view that even if the wife is working the decision making power lies with the husbands only and this shows that the women's position is only secondary in the process of decision making of their families.

Extent of sexual exploitation on the construction site: Not many respondents were open to this questions and it was found that only 32.34 per cent of the respondents agreed that the women workers on the site are either looked down or are harassed physically, verbally and emotionally. And 14.46 per cent of the respondents replied in negative and said there was no harassment on the site. It was hardly surprising that 53.2 per cent did not respond and declined to discuss this issue as they were afraid, embarrassed and also scared of social stigma to answer this question asked by the researcher. As per ILO clause there is no provision from *mukadam* regarding safety of women workers from sexual harassment. Due to fear of both husband and wife losing their job majority women do not lodge complaint. On the basis of the information collected it can be understood, that sexual exploitation, harassment is there prevailing among construction women workers but to what extent cannot be pin pointed. During data collection through the interview the respondents have given the information regarding sexual harrassement at the workplace. They were hesitant/shy to answer correctly or freely , but during informal talk womens spoke about their fear and helplessness. Section 509 of the Indian Penal Code, prohibits any word, gesture or act intended to insult the modesty of a women. Under the IPC, sexual harrassement has been dealt with as criminal offence. During research it was observed that the women workers at workplace has to tolerate sexually coloured remarks, unwelcomed physical, verbal or nonverbal conducts of sexual nature.

The data on awareness among the women construction workers about the trade union aspects show that majority of the women workers were neither interested nor aware of any trade union operating in their area. During the survey, almost all (95.6%) women workers replied in negative when they were asked about trade union of their area. 96.34 per cent respondents expressed disinterest in knowing and in participating in trade union activities.

On the whole the analysis in this chapter highlights that these workers come from the poorer socio-economic backgrounds as the migrant workforce and live on the construction site itself.. Almost majority of them are either from schedule caste and schedule tribes earning very meager amount that is not always enough to support their families. The life of these women workers is very tough because of the double burden of working at home as well as at the work site. Lack of basic amenities like toilets, potable adequate water or electricity adds to the difficulties list. Unnatural lifestyle, no privacy or safety, running kitchen without storage facility and kerosene at higher price are also some of the difficulties faced by these women. These women hardly get any time for recreation or leisure activities.

They have to perform a dual role relating to production and reproduction. While they carry the primary responsibility of bearing and rearing children, they are invariably involved in economic activities also. Negligence of health, lack of medical facilities mainly during delivery ,gender violence and exploitation at work are burdens which are compounded because of poverty, illiteracy and dependency on others. The burdens are heavy and there are no visible respites. These women are unprotected and suffer from economic exploitation due to their ignorance and illiteracy. Basic right to vote, ration card not available adds to their plight. There are many laws which helps to safeguard the rights of women but are not implemented because of ignorance and illiteracy.

Human rights violation are very high in informal sector with respect to Minimum Wage Act, Equal Remuneration Act, Contract Labour Act, Safe Working Condition, Insurance and Provident Fund Act, Fixed work Timing, Maternity Benefits Acts etc.

REFERENCES

1. Chaudhari, K.K., *History of Bombay*, Modern Period Gazetteers Dept., Govt. of Maharashtra, Mumbai, 1987.
2. *Op. cit.*
3. Government of India, *Census of India* 2001, GOI, New Delhi, 2001.

Suggestions and Conclusion

On the basis of data analysed in the course of the research carried out it can be concluded that many of the labour legislations are not being properly implemented at the sampled construction site. The life of these women construction workers on the sampled site portrays that there is an urgent need to make some suitable amendments in the existing labour legislations and has to be effectively implemented.

The discrimination faced by women worker in the labour market is substantiated by the study conducted on women worker in construction industry. However there exist a wide gap between the goals enunciated in the Constitution, legislation, policies, plans, programmes, and related mechanisms on the one hand and the situational reality of the status of women in India, on the other.

- In the Indian scenario, in this male dominated society women are regarded as performing a subordinate role and they are to supplement the efforts of their male counterparts in society. And so therefore even in regard to employment women stand at the bottom of the hierarchy doing unskilled work doing the most arduous work of lifting and head loading construction material and carrying it by negotiating flimsy and risky ladders and pathways. While men in unskilled work are able to pick up skills on the job and move up in the hierarchy, women are seldom given opportunities for mobility in employment .It was found by the researcher that all the women in the sample were doing unskilled arduous jobs.

Even though the practice of taking advance is illegal according to the Bonded Labour Act, 1976 the practice continues as it is evident from the research conducted at this particular site.

- Two types of recruitment methods are followed to recruit the families of women workers at the construction site. One type of recruitment was the women workers and their families were directly or indirectly known to the mukadam or some other staff members of the site and the second method was employing those workers who are not known to them. These workers are recruited through a intermediary. He acts as a surety for the money advanced to these workers during the time of recruitment. The women workers were noticed to have a very limited role in the entire process of recruitment as majority of them simply agree to the decision taken by their male counterparts. But as observed to the study, the conclusion derived over here is the procedures of recruitment as laid down in various legislations especially in the Contract Act, 1970 is not followed.

  The study at the site revealed that the type of work to be performed and the criteria of wage determination depended on the sex of the worker. The data revealed that separate wage rates and work involvement are fixed for females and males in this industry. The fixed wages for women for eight hours a day is Rs. 80 per day as compared to men who earned Rs. 120 to 150 according to their skills and work. If they worked more than the statutory timing they were paid overtime on an hourly basis. The wages were paid after every fortnight and the women's earnings were handed over to her husband and as a result the female workers have to depend on their husbands for even for the money that they earned.

- The field study revealed that workers were given leave after every fortnight on the amavasya day as the owner believes on a superstition that no construction work should be done at the site on that day. However, on days of such enforced holidays none of the workers are paid wages. This is a violation of the right to paid holidays. Due to illiteracy, 96.34 per cent of the women workers in these construction sites were not aware of any trade union operating in their area nor were they interested in trade union activities as they felt that participation in the trade union activities is the job of their male counterparts. Secondly, these women construction workers hardly have any time to involve themselves in trade union activities as they have to perform dual responsibilities of helping their husband in work and performing domestic chores. At the construction site the worker have no contact with any NGOs In spite of a number of laws purporting to provide basic social security benefits relating to old age, marriage sickness, injury and death to the workers in the unorganised sector, the gains have been only marginal particularly in case of women workers in construction industry. The existing social security schemes have not been able to provide security to the workers because of the non-implementation of these schemes by the owner of the construction site.
- Women workers on the construction site under study were ignorant of the labour legislations. No women

in the sample was aware of the legislations like The Maternity Benefit Act 1961, The ESI Act 1948, The Interstate Migrants Workers Act 1979, The Factories Act 1948 etc. Even the civil society organisations do not seem to have educated women in this aspect.

- The periodic shifting of the construction workers is one of the main reason that the workers of this industry face various problems regarding regularising their employment, implementation of labour laws and availability of better housing facilities. The owners feel that as these workers have to shift once the construction is over, it is not financially viable for them to make well furnished houses, crèches, canteens and other such things.

Suggestions

- The Government should immediately implement the Acts that they have enacted.
- Government should constitute a tripartite committee every year at the state level to decide about the rates of wages, the bonus, and the incentives for these workers. Efforts should also be made by the enforcement machinery to effectively implement the recommendations of this committee. Role of the trade unions and the NGO's in this connection is recommended.
- Under the supervision of the state level tripartite committee, a Common Welfare Fund must be constituted with the help of the contributions from the workers, employers, and the Government. The fund can be used for the pension, health, insurance and other facilities like loans etc. But this initiative cannot be successful unless the workers of this industry are regularized or given some service cards. The State Government should also make provisions

to compensate these workers against natural disasters like heavy rains, floods, cyclones and fires etc.

- Voluntary Organizations and trade unions can work towards making improvements in their health status, educational attainments and general welfare. These groups should give special attention to the following areas:
  (*a*) To organize awareness programmes regarding their legal rights, health, and nutrition and sanitation;
  (*b*) To make arrangement for doctors to organize health camps or free medical check-ups;
  (*c*) To make provisions of schools/tutors for the children of these workers.
- The employers should make efforts to provide them better living facilities provided with some arrangements relating to kitchen, bathroom and latrines.
- Last but not the least , the Government should give a considerable attention to the construction industry and the problems of its workers and employees as the industry provides a pivotal support to all developmental activities relating to buildings and constructions in the country.

Conclusion

The present study observes that there is an urgent need to make suitable amendments in the existing labour legislations so far as the construction industry is concerned. This industry has some unique characteristics and therefore it is practically not possible to cover all the aspects of the industry by the present forms of many of the existing labour laws. The construction industry is different than other industries, *firstly*, because of the fact that the living arrangement of its workers and their work places are in the same surroundings. *Secondly*, all the operations incidental to construction are done in groups consisting usually of the family members of these workers. Therefore the workers have to live with their families in the close vicinity of their workplaces. *Thirdly* the most unique feature is that the job of these workers are temporary in nature as they have to search for other jobs or move to other construction site owned by the same employee.

Bibliography

Agarwal, Bina and Floro, Mario, *Women's Work in the World Economy*, MacMillan Publication, London, 1992.

Bannerjee, Nirmala, *Women Workers in the Unorganized Sector*, Sangam Books, Hyderabad, India, 1985.

Banerjee, Nirmala, Why *They Get A Worse Deal*, Siddhi Publishers, Hyderabad, 1989.

Bagchi, K. K., and Gope, N., *State, Labour and Development – An Indian Prespective*, Abhijeet Publication, New Delhi, 2008.

Bentham, J., "*Anarchial Fallacies*". Melden, A. (Ed.), *Human Rights*, Belmont, California, Wadsworth, 1970.

Bhattacharya, Damyant, *Invisible Hands: Status of Women's Work in India*, Women Networking, Mumbai, 2004.

Bremen, Jan, *Footloose Labour Working in India's Informal Economy*, Cambridge University Press, Cambridge, 1996.

Brysk Alison (Ed), *Globalisation and Human Rights*, University of California Press, Berkely, 2002 .

Chauhan O.P., and Dealwal, Lalit, *HumanRights Promotion and Protection*, Anmol Publisher, New Delhi, 2004.

Chauhan, P., *Women Labour in India*, V.V.Giri National Labour Institute, Noida, 2007.

Claude, R. P., and Burns, H.W. (Eds.), *Human Rights in the World Community: Issues and Action,* University of Pennsylvania Press, Philadelphia, 1989.

Coicaud, Jean Marc and *et.al., Globalisation of Human Rights,* Rawat Publications, Jaipur, 2004.

Creevey, Lucy, *Changing Women's Lives and Work: An Analysis of Impacts of Eight Micro Enterprise Project,* the Intermediate Technology, London, 1996.

Dak, T. M., *Women and Work in Indian Society,* Discovery Publishing House, Delhi, 1988.

Datar, Chaya, *Women's Labour Bearer of Patriarchy – An Indian Experience,* Tata Institute of Social Sciences, Mumbai, 1996.

Everett, Jana, and Savara, Mira, *Women and Organisation in the Informal Sector,* Himalaya Publishing House, Mumbai,1996.

Gandhi, Nandita, and Shah, Nandita, *Shadow Workers Women in Home-based Production,* Himalaya Publication, Mumbai, 1992.

"Gender Role Beliefs and Stress in Working Women", *Urdhva Mula,* Vol. 1, No. 1, November 2002, pp. 63-65.

Huws, Ursula, *Action Programme for the Protection of Home-based Workers : Ten Case Studies Around the World,* International Labour Organisation, Geneva, 1995.

ILO, *Employment, Income, Equality: A Strategy For Increasing Productivity Employment In Kenya,* ILO, Geneva, 1972.

ILO-WEP, *Informal Sector and Urban Employment: A Review of Activities in the Urban Informal Sector, International Labour Office, and Geneva,* 1990.

Jeanne, Frances I., and Jaime, B. Polo, *Fishers, Traders, Farmers, Wives : The Life Stories of Ten Women in a Fishing Village,* Institute of Philippine Culture, Manila, 1992.

Joshi, Mahesh V., *Women Rural Labourers: Problems and Prospects,* APH Publishing Corporation, New Delhi, 1999.

Lakkineni, Ratna Kumari, *Economic Discrimination against Women,* Abhijeet Publications, New Delhi, 2008.

Levin, Lech, *Human Rights: Questions and Answers,* National Book Trust/ UNESCO, India Mumbai, 1998.

Mallya Sudha Laxman : *Socio-economic Condition of Women Workers In Construction Industry.* M.Phil Dissertation, Tamil Nadu, 2008

Mandal, B.B., *Strategies for Empowering Women in Unorganised Sector with Special Reference To Bihar,* Inter India Publication, New Delhi, 1997.

Mitha, Yameena, *Building Your Dreams: Women in the Construction Industry*, Applied Economic Social Research, Lahore, 1989.

Murthy, S., *Women And Development*, RBSA Publishers, Jaipur, 2001.

Muthuraja C., *Women Folk in Indian Agriculture : An Analysis of Their Participation and Contribution*, Intellectual Publishing House, New Delhi, 1997.

Pachouly, M., "We have to Compromise Somewhere", *Times of India*, 20th August, 2002.

Pande, P. N., and Papola, T. S., *Women Khadi Workers: A Study of Economic Conditions and Status of Women Spinners in U.P.*, Giri Institute of Development Studies, Lucknow,1985.

Papola, T. S., *Urban Informal Sector in Developing Economy*, Vikas Publications, New Delhi, 1981.

Patel, Vibhuti, *Feminist Jurisprudence-Contemporary Concerns*, Majlis, Mumbai, 2002.

Progamme of Women and Economical, Social and Cultural Rights (PWESCR)- *Partnering Organisation*, Nehru Enclave , New Delhi, 2008

Saksena, A., *Implementation of the Convention on the Elimination of Discrimination Against Women (CEDAW) in India with Reference to Women Workers*, Report submitted to the Department of Civics and Politics, University of Mumbai under the University Grants Commission's Department Special Assistance Programme, 2003.

Sethuraman, S. V., *The Urban Informal Sector in Developing Countries: Employment Poverty and Environment*, International Labour Organisation, Geneva, 1981.

Schenk, Sandbergen, *Women and Seasonal Labour Migration*, Sage Publications, Delhi, 1995.

Singh, A. N., *Women Domestic Workers: Socio-economic Life*, Shipra Publications, Delhi, 2001.

Singh, D. P., *Women Workers in Unorganised Sector*, Deep and Deep Publication, New Delhi, 2005.

South Asia Human rights Documentation Centre, *Handbook of Human Rights and Criminal Justice in India: System and Procedure*, Oxford University Press, N. Delhi, 2006.

Thara, Bhai, *Women's Studies in India*, A P H Publishing Corporation, New Delhi, 2000.

Yin-Shin, *The Way to Buddhism*, Wisdom Publications, Somerville, 2006.

Index